Lessons
I'm Going To
Teach My Kids
Too Late

Lessons I'm Going To Teach My Kids Too Late

Brad Yung

CIP DATA TO FOLLOW

For Harry,

without whom this book
would have been
finished much sooner,
but there would have been
nothing to write about

Lessons

Lessons I'm Going To Teach My Kids Too Late

18. He that hath no CHILDREN
doth bring them up well 37

19. CLEAN your room 39

20. Those who can, DO. Those who can't, teach. 41

21. IMITATION is the sincerest form of flattery 43

22. Be PROUD of where you come from 45

23. Don't JUDGE a book by its cover 46

24. If you can't say somethin' NICE,
don't say nothin' at all 48

25. It's WEIRD not to be weird 50

26. Keep your SECRETS safe.................................... 52

27. If you want the RAINBOW,
you gotta put up with the rain 54

28. A ROLLING stone gathers no moss 55

29. It's nice to be IMPORTANT, but it's more
important to be nice 57

30. Actions speak louder than words 58

31. Nothing GOLD can stay 61

32. WATCH your step 62

33. ROCK the boat.. 64

34. Get INVOLVED 66

35. You're never too old
to LEARN something new 68

36. You can't TEACH an old dog new tricks................ 70

37. Old FRIENDS are best... 71

38. Little SAID is soonest mended............................. 73

39. Children should be SEEN and not heard 74

Lessons I'm Going To Teach My Kids Too Late

Foreword

I first met writer and illustrator Brad Yung when he was working undercover, dressed like a man employed at a toy shop. We were in a toy shop but don't let that fool you, he was always incognito, the Crazy Genius studying the underbelly of absurdity of which the most discerning of minds had already been fooled into thinking was this other plain thing called reality.

At the time, many people in the city believed that his weekly comic strip was, well, a weekly comic strip, but those of us who knew the truth understood the secret messages he conveyed to the deepest parts of our lizard brains. There was always too much genius coming out of Brad Yung's mind to let it flow out in full stream.

Now Yung has advice for raising your children and, make no mistake, it is also a conspiracy, another series of disruptions from the mind of a gifted writer who is so cool that no one really knows who he is and he's okay with that. "Ignore the writer and love the writing" is one of the messages I've decoded when running the algorithm on his particular act of illusion and self-deprecating wisdom.

Like the finest works of Shaun Tan, Yung is not constricted by normalcy, predictability, or a need to explain why he thinks he has a right to alter your understanding of reality and childhood. He just does it with something that sometimes resembles magic but other times resembles a psychotic and gritty self-help manifesto.

Sometimes Yung writes like a haiku master, sometimes like a guy who worked at a toy shop, and sometimes like a secret agent trained in psychological warfare who has been tasked to rewire your brain so that your life can, for a moment, unravel with a clear view of the absurd.

These lessons of parenthood are written as they should be, with the skill of a sage and the imagination of a devious child who refused to conform, refused to give up on the life of the imagination, and instead made it his mission to pierce holes in not only what we've been told is the correct way to raise children, but what we've been told is the correct way to view the world.

Brad Yung was not his mother's favourite child and it shows. But there is still hope. He can be one of your favourite writers. Trust me that with this book, he will be.

Brad Cran
Vancouver Poet Laureate, 2009–2011

Preface

LESSON

0

THOUGHT

W hen I was much younger than I am now, I received a children's book as a present. It was something about a mouse, I think. It didn't leave any impression on me except the Preface. The author of the book had a young daughter and was dissatisfied with the selection of children's books available to read to her at bedtime, so he wrote his own.

However, he was not an accomplished writer nor a fast one, so by the time he had finished the book, his daughter was all grown up and he didn't read to her at bedtime anymore. I remember thinking, *What an ungrateful child.* She couldn't indulge an old man? She didn't have to let him tuck her in or read the entire thing to her — how about just one chapter, for old times' sake? She could at least, at the very least, read the damn book herself, the one he wrote for her over the course of at least a decade. Disgusted, I threw the book aside and never read it.

It took me twelve years to write the book you hold in your hands right now. I started it before I had kids, before I even thought I'd ever have kids. But now that I do, I'm certainly not going to read it to them. In fact, I'm going to hide it from them. I don't want them to know it even exists. They'll find out about it as adults, by accident, when they find a copy in a dollar bin at a used bookstore somewhere, presuming there are any bookstores left.

I hope you like this book. I hope you read past the Preface. I hope it makes an impression. I hope you bought it, I hope you buy multiple copies and give them to friends and family and acquaintances, then they do the same, and so on and so on.

Because when my kids finally do find out about this book and read it, then think back over their lives and everything we ever did together, I anticipate massive lawsuits.

But at least they'll have read it.

LESSON 0
IT'S THE THOUGHT THAT COUNTS

1

CURIOUS

I want to buy a house
And build a secret room in it
And not tell the kids about it
Until we've moved out.

It would just come up in casual conversation one day.

"Oh, we kept that stuff in the secret room."

"What secret room?" they'd ask.

"The one in the old house on Elm Street."

"Oh my god! Where was it?"

"Just off of the living room. You'd pull a certain book out of the bookshelf and the whole case would swing out, revealing the hidden room."

"That sounds so cool!"

"It was."

"Why didn't you ever tell us about it?"

"Well, obviously, because we didn't want you going in there."

"What was in it?"

"Stuff we didn't want you to know about. Birthday presents, valuables, alcohol..."

"Aw," they'd say, "we wish we had known about it."
"Well then, you should have spent more of your childhood looking for it, tapping on the walls, jiggling the fixtures, and pushing on all the rocks in the fireplace."
Like I did.

LESSON 1

BE CURIOUS ABOUT THE WORLD AROUND YOU

LESSON

2

STRIVE

"**W**hy can't you be more like Bobby?"

Bobby was the kid two doors down who was, evidently, perfect. He was polite, well-behaved, the best son in the history of good sons.

"He's so obedient."

"You make him sound like a dog."

He spat when he talked, had a really bad bowl haircut, wore the tackiest thrift-store clothing and cried at the first sign of discomfort. On his 16th birthday, he found out his uncle was actually his real father and that was why his other father hated him. Years of abuse finally made sense. He stopped crying so much, but he didn't smile anymore, either.

"Why can't you be more like Gordon?"

Gordon was the kid who destroyed the curve. Straight A's, top of the class, won all the scholarships.

"You have to study more, then you could catch up."

"I can't. I'm falling asleep *walking to school*."

He had coke-bottle glasses, a creepy laugh, arrogance to spare, and the world's worst posture. In his third year of university, he was caught hacking into the school's mainframe. His defence in court was that the security was so poor that it wasn't really hacking. Virtually unemployable after his expulsion, he maintains his innocence to this day.

"Why can't you be more like Danny?"
  Kind, generous, helpful, and compliant.
  "Danny's so good, never any trouble."
      "Danny's never anything."
  He let his parents control his life, make all his decisions for him. They told him what to wear, what to eat, what to do, when to do it. He just turned forty and still lives at home, huddled in the cold basement surrounded by years of old newspapers, clipping coupons, and watching TV.

My kids will never hear the phrase, "Why can't you be more like..." I'm not going to compare them to other kids. They'll stand alone, comfortable and confident, no insecurity or doubt tracking their steps. I want them to grow up happy, humble, and out of the house.

And that's where they'll find out they've got a lot of catching up to do.

LESSON 2

STRIVE TO BE A BETTER PERSON

3

EDUCATION

Just before he died, my grandfather gave my mother a homemade, handwritten book containing our family history. Unable to read Chinese, I asked my mother who our ancestors were and what they had done.

"They were mostly scholars," she said.

Mostly scholars.

That is exactly not what a young boy wants to hear. A young boy wants to hear that his ancestors were at least remarkable. Great explorers, perhaps, or pioneers of something. To know that he is descended from brave and fearless warriors is to know that some of that heroic blood may be coursing through his veins, that he too may be destined to do great and heroic things someday.

Mostly scholars.

I'm descended from people with book-smarts. My ancestors went to school and studied various topics in the library. Maybe they became authoritative experts in some field and dispensed knowledge to younger students.

And so, like them, I went to school and studied hard, then went on to higher learning. And, as I grew older, I gradually pried more stories from my mother's loosening grasp.

There was my father, who died when I was very young, who came over when he was twelve and lived in Vancouver's Chinatown when it was still walled off and dangerous. He was part of the gang of Chinese kids who protected it, using secret calls and whistles to alert the others that the white kids had come down to make trouble again. Gather the troops and drive them out!

There was my great-uncle Loy, who taught hand-to-hand combat to Canadian soldiers during World War II. A martial artist so accomplished, there wasn't a belt black enough for him. To harden his hands, he would slap a brick every day — his hands were as tough as leather and the brick was smooth all over and half the size it had been when he started. If a Chinese family anywhere in Canada was having racial problems in their community, they could write Loy and he would travel to their town and try to negotiate a peace. Failing that, he would beat up their tormentors, warning them that if there were any more problems, he would come back and beat them up again.

And there was my grandfather, a poet and a dreamer. His wife hated him and his lack of ambition, his idiotic musings and his worthless writings. He would see a leaf fall in the backyard and then spend a whole afternoon composing a poem about it. When he died, as is the custom, his wife burned all his possessions, probably with glee. The homemade, handwritten book is the only thing that he wrote that still exists and it's probably not his best work.

Mostly scholars.

Here, son. My grandfather gave this book to my mother, she gave it to me, and now I'm giving it to you. I have no idea what it says exactly, but it contains our family history. Apparently, your great-great-great-great-grandfather was a pirate or something. Pretty cool, huh?

LESSON 3

NOTHING IS MORE IMPORTANT THAN A GOOD EDUCATION

LESSON

4

RISKS

My friend in high school had a dad who was a total nerd. He fit the stereotype perfectly — engineer, really smart, poor fashion sense, coke-bottle glasses, bad posture, the works. We liked him because he helped us with our homework, but we made light fun of him behind his back. But not too much — we were nerds too.

One winter day, he was driving his wife and teenage sons home in the family station wagon. It was the middle of a light snowstorm with maybe half an inch on the ground, a lot for Vancouver. His wife was freaking out.

"Be careful, there's snow on the road! It's slippery!"

"What, this?" he replied.

He jerked the wheel and turned the car sideways.

"This? This is nothing."

He hit the accelerator around the curve until they got to their street. He whipped the wheel the other way, neatly swinging the car around into the opposite direction.

They slid up to their driveway, where he expertly manoeuvred the car around again, skidding to a stop perfectly aligned in their parking spot. He calmly got out of the car, leaving his gape-mouthed family behind in stunned silence.

Turns out, when he was younger, living in Ottawa, he was an ice racer, one of those crazy guys who waits for the lake to freeze so he can get an old beater car and race other crazy guys around on top of it. Nerd Dad had this insanely awesome skill and nobody knew — not his wife, not his kids. He went from dork to Coolest Dad Ever and it was all his sons could talk about the next day at school.

Now, I'm no ice racer. I think I can do some cool stuff, but I don't know if any of it would impress you. Which I'm going to want to do at some point when you're a sneering, sarcastic teenager. It doesn't have to be anything big, just something to temporarily break the veneer of disdain you're going to put on when you get to that age.

So then I can remember, if just for a brief moment, how you used to look up at me... like you do now.

LESSON 4

DON'T TAKE UNNECESSARY RISKS

LESSON
5

CHANGE

There's an old saying: "Give me a child until he is seven and I will give you the man." Essentially, it means that children's personalities and futures are pretty much set by the time they're seven years old. My son, at the moment of this writing, is five.

I'm feeling the pressure.

I try to think back to what I was like at seven. I imagine I was much like I am now: shy, quiet, anxious, lazy, introverted, worried, unfocussed, and a little weird.

Then I look at my son and I see so many of the same qualities. I can't help but be concerned. I have good qualities too, as does my son, but if he wasn't quite so much like me, perhaps he could have a better life or at least an easier time of it.

I'm conflicted. Should I intentionally mould him into whom I think he should be or just let him develop organically? Other people try to shape their kids, show them right from wrong, set them up for their futures. But where do you stop? I don't want to be too controlling, like the jock dad forcing his son into sports, but I don't want him to drift aimlessly, either.

My mom definitely tried to push me in certain directions, but they just weren't me. I finally rebelled in my twenties, but it was so late, I didn't know how to go about getting what I wanted because I'd never actually asked myself what that was. I know she was well-intentioned, so I comfort myself with the thought that if I'd done what she wanted me to, I'd still be dissatisfied with my life, just for different reasons.

I want my son to be happy, to be who he wants to be, and that might be vastly different from who I think he should be or what I want him to be, if those are even two separate things.

I want to be happy. I try to be who I want to be, but I don't know how or even what that is sometimes.

Going by the saying, I've got about two years to figure it out. I'm pretty sure that's not enough time. It's probably for the best.

LESSON 5

THE LEOPARD DOES NOT CHANGE HIS SPOTS

LESSON

6

VALUE

Another school day, another damn special art project.

Don't get me wrong. I love that my kids are learning how to be creative and how to express themselves in different mediums: drawings and paintings, sculptures from clay, ribbons, macaroni, papier-mâché, buttons and baubles and things made from wood, puppets and models — and everything's good. But there's so much of it...

The fridge door is full. The fireplace mantel is overflowing, just like every windowsill in every room of the house. My office desk is covered with cards and mementoes and special rocks and decorated shells "just for you, Daddy." Am I supposed to be keeping all this stuff?

I like the drawings — they're flat and store easily. The paintings are nice, too. The paper-plate turkey might get just a bit flattened, but I cannot guarantee the solar system mobile's safety at all. Some of the rocks are pretty, but a lot of it is just gravel you've brought home for some reason. And this thing today — seriously, it's just a stick with glitter glued to it. Do I have to treasure it forever?

I asked my mom what she kept of my stuff. It was less than the contents of a shoebox: a plaster cast of my hand, a cross-stitch belt she never wore, and a wooden spoon I carved in workshop. The rest all got chucked. And you know, I was relieved. I would have been mortified if she'd hung onto that crap, fawning over it and going on about the various arts and crafts I was forced to do.

Your mother is in charge of enthusiasm. She's the one who can dredge up excitement over every single thing you create. Me, I need something a bit more spectacular. I need something that's going to wow me. Your mother framed your napkin doodle. I would have wiped my mouth with it and thrown it in the trash.

Please understand — I love all your little art projects, but just for a short while, unless they're really, really good. I don't mean to hurt your feelings, but you can do better and the lesser stuff has to fall by the wayside.

Think of it like parenting. Some days I'll be good at it and some days I'm going to suck at it.

Like today, perhaps.

LESSON 6

THE FREE MARKET DICTATES VALUE

LESSON

7

SQUEAKY

I believe I've inherited my mother's penchant for complaining about everything. I'm pretty sure she got it from her mother, but I don't know if my grandmother got it from her mother or if she just had a lot to complain about. But listening to the two of them talking whenever they were together, which was often, you'd think there was nothing right in the world.

They complained about politicians and the news of the day. They complained about family members and friends. They complained about the weather, last night's dinner, last week's dinner, or the kids on the street making too much noise. Again.

The angrier and more frustrated they got, the louder they became. Their faces would contort and crinkle up, a physical indicator of their intensely personal, deeply-felt pain. It would bounce back and forth between them, magnifying and echoing off each other, while my sister and I sat there and absorbed it all, I guess.

My wife says I complain too much. I always thought I was quite the optimist, but perhaps only in comparison to my mother and grandmother.

My grandmother's gone now, which means my mom has nobody

to sound off against on a regular basis. So whenever I call her, it reliably devolves into a prolonged complaint session. And it's the same complaints as last time, the same as last year, the same as I've been hearing all my life.

I'm trying to complain less for my kids' sakes. I know it's unattractive and nobody wants to hear that crap all the time, and I want them to have something else going for them that I didn't. It's hard when there's so much wrong with the world and so much to complain about, but I really don't want to make that their main impression of how things are or how they should be.

I want them to be genuinely optimistic about the world. I want them to be full of awe and wonder and eagerness to explore. I want them to know about kindness and beauty and all the amazing experiences that are out there waiting for them. I have no idea where to tell them to start looking.

I wish my mom and grandmother hadn't been so negative. I wish they'd actually done something about their problems instead of just complaining all the time. I'm trying not to go with my initial instincts, to find the positives in every situation, but it's so difficult to break my programming. I worry that I'm too late, that I didn't catch it in time, or enough of the time, and my kids are going to be whiny complainers like me, like my mom, like my grandmother.

If they do turn out like that, I'll try not to complain about it too much. That would be hypocritical and redundant and self-defeating. And while I'm all those things, I do want better for my kids and I think it can be done.

I guess that's just the optimist in me talking.

LESSON 7

THE SQUEAKY WHEEL GETS THE GREASE

8

MODERATION

My wife and I are having a fight in the car. You would think the topic of your favourite colour would be argument-proof, but you would be wrong.

"How can your favourite colour be purple?" she argues. "All your clothes are blue!"

"I don't need to see it all the time," I reply. "And I do have one purple shirt."

"Which you hardly ever wear! It's not your favourite shirt!"

"But I would only see it if I was looking down."

"You have no other purple things!"

"Well, I don't want to overdo it."

There are many things I like, but I moderate them. I don't eat my favourite food very often because I wouldn't want to grow tired of it. I watch my favourite movie only every few years. It's a treat for me, something special. I've read my favourite book exactly once. I'm saving that repeat experience for a later time.

My wife does her favourite things over and over. She watches the same movies repeatedly, sometimes just days after the last viewing. She eats her favourite foods so much, she gets sick of them. And most of her clothes are green, her favourite colour.

I look back and smile at the kids in the back seat.

"Actually, my favourite colours are blue and red. But you can only have one favourite colour, so I combined them into purple."

"You can't do that!" my wife explodes. "That's the stupidest thing I've ever heard!"

She's really angry now and has stopped talking to me.

We fight about a lot of stupid things. Sometimes I'm right, sometimes I'm wrong. In either case, I like to hold my ground. I'll make up weird reasons or justifications — the stranger the excuse, the angrier she gets. How can my favourite colour be wrong? How can she think my favourite colour is wrong?

I know, I know. I probably shouldn't wind her up like that so often, but I do enjoy it so.

LESSON 8

MODERATION IN ALL THINGS

LESSON

9

MONEY

The young girl is at Sunday brunch with her family in the booth next to ours in the modest family-oriented eatery. She's had her pancakes and she drew on her placemat with crayons, her little collection of toy cars carefully arranged on the windowsill beside her. And now she wants to play the claw machine.

Three weak-springed hooks hang over a motley collection of ratty stuffed toys. At a dollar a play, the machine probably makes money even if you win. The trick is not to try for the toy you want, but the toy on top. Combine a very short time limit on the claw with a young girl's lack of hand-eye coordination and she's quickly lost the three dollars her family was willing to give up.

Back at the table, she pleads for more money. Her mother looks through her purse, not too thoroughly.

"Oh, that was all the change I had."

The girl persists, she begins to whine, so the father steps in.

"It's a scam."

The girl doesn't understand.

"It's a scam," the father repeats, more emphatically.

"I don't think she knows what the word 'scam' means," the mother suggests.

"It means you'll never win. You can keep putting money in it forever and ever and you'll never get anything out of it. You can never win. It's a rip-off, a scam."

The girl's face is frozen, her mouth slightly agape, her eyes actually losing sparkle. She's looking straight ahead at neither her father nor her mother, but at something far off in the distance, past them, past the horizon. Her little brain ticks over, absorbing this new, unwanted, and unwarranted information. You can almost see her dreams shattering, her awe and wonder at the world collapsing like a ratty stuffed toy falling from a weak-springed hook's tentative grasp.

Done with breakfast, they pay their bill and tip poorly, recouping their loss.

"Don't forget your cars."

"Do you want the drawing you made?"

No, she doesn't need it, not where she's going. Home to get the "you die, you turn to dust" speech.

I want to stop her on her way out. I want to grab her little arm and shake her and tell her that you *can* win on that machine. That I've seen it with my own eyes, that it *is* possible. That *anything* is possible. But I don't.

We need her. We need people like her, people like she's going to be, to offset my kids. Someone's got to balance out the dreamers, the optimists, the ones who don't get the soul-crushing speech, the ones who don't know there are limits on anything, the ones who don't even realize that they could ever fail.

And when they do, I'll go down into the basement, and haul out an old, dust-covered box full of ratty stuffed toys and I'll wave them in their faces.

"Should have put the money into a savings plan, you dummies."

And they'll make an appointment with the girl and go to her office and have a long talk with her about what their options are and how to ensure their financial security and what investment plan is best for them and so on, and so on, and so on, until their eyes look just like hers.

LESSON 9
PUT SOME MONEY ASIDE FOR A RAINY DAY

LESSON
10

WAR

I am clearly not my mother's favourite child. This has been painfully obvious my entire life. It used to bug me, but these things happen and I'm okay with it now.

I was the oldest. I should have been the most capable, the most independent — and in a way I was. Emotionally unavailable and socially inept, academically gifted but ignorant in the ways of the world, I suppose I was too much my mother's opposite. And with so many expectations I failed to fulfill, I guess I was also the biggest disappointment.

My sister was the youngest, the baby of the family, more well-rounded, and a girl. They could talk about anything because they had so much more in common. I must have been as alien to them as they were to me. And with me being so angry all the time, it's no wonder they shied away.

So now I have children of my own, an eldest son and a baby daughter, and I'm trying really hard not to, but I have a favourite. I love them both, but I can relate to one more than the other, and that's all it takes, I guess.

My wife is the classic middle child of three — an older brother and a younger sister — so she knows exactly what it's like, how it is. Luckily, our little family has the same number of parents as kids and, though my wife will never admit it, it's pretty clear she has a favourite, too. And wouldn't you know, it's the opposite of mine, but for the same reasons as me.

The kids are still young, so maybe they haven't picked up on any of it yet. Or maybe they're smarter than we think, or we're not as smart as we think, and they've already figured out how it's going to be. Maybe they're okay with it, since it seems pretty balanced. Or maybe they're not and resentments are already brewing, insecurities already growing over questions of their self-worth, their sense of their own likeability and lovability.

But I don't want to discuss it with them, not just yet, in case they don't already know. I don't want to break their little hearts. I don't think I could handle it.

I'll let their mother do it — she can handle it, they can handle hearing it from her. Especially since I just found out that they both favour her over me.

But I'm okay with it. No, really, I am.

LESSON 10

ALL'S FAIR IN LOVE AND WAR

11

GROW

I kept all my old toys.

Seriously, all of them. Well, not the baby stuff, but pretty much everything else that came later that wasn't completely broken. And I took fairly good care of my toys, so it's a lot.

Boxes and boxes of toy cars and trucks and planes and trains and track, stickers and stuffed animals and puzzles, building bricks and plastic trinkets from gumball machines, poorly assembled model kits and comics and half-finished activity books — I kept it all.

I kept it under the pretence that I would give it to my kids one day, even when it didn't look like I would ever have any. That was the justification each time I moved them, then stored them, then moved them again and stored them again.

Really, honestly, I was just clinging to my childhood. I didn't want to give it up. I didn't want to have to be an adult and do adult things and take on adult responsibilities and do adult this and adult that. And I didn't even play with the toys — I just kept them, looking at them every once in a while and reminiscing.

And when I finally had kids, I went into my collection and selected some of my toys, presenting them with some small amount of show and flourish.

"These are the toys I used to play with when I was your age."

And they looked at me with blank, mercifully short stares. Then, they went back to playing with their new, shiny toys, leaving my old, dingy ones where I'd placed them.

Yes, it was heartbreaking. How could they not like the toys I'd loved and played with for so many of my childhood hours? Was there something wrong with them? With me? Was I seeing them through the sparkling haze of nostalgia? The rest of my collection stayed in their boxes for a while longer.

I recently tried again, but I was a little more careful with my selection. This time it was a hit and we played with them together on the floor for hours. Me and my memories, them and their newfound discoveries.

I'll be going through my old toys again and handing them over. Hit or miss, I have to not take it personally. They're going to like what they like and I can't fault them for it, just like my mom couldn't have expected me to like every toy she ever bought me.

Because even though I didn't love all my toys, I still kept them. Because I didn't know which ones my kids would enjoy. Because I knew if I threw any of it away, I'd regret it. Because, despite some early tragedy, I had a happy childhood and I want my kids to be happy as well.

And if my old toys can make them happy and their new toys make them happy and if the lot of us sitting on the floor playing together makes us one happy little family, then I'll have succeeded and it'll have all been worth it.

You see boxes of clutter and a sad man clinging to his childhood, I see smiles on my kids' faces mirroring my own. And who wouldn't want to cling to that?

LESSON 11

THERE IS A TIME TO GROW UP AND LEAVE CHILDISH THINGS BEHIND

LESSON

12

SPEAK

I don't want to be the kind of dad that screams at his kids. And I certainly don't want to be the kind of dad whose kids scream at him.

Go to your room. Count to ten. Take a walk around the block. Then, if you're still angry, take another one. Then we'll talk.

It's all good advice. Things can be said in anger and they can't be taken back. You can apologize, but the words were still uttered, the heart was still stabbed.

So here's what we're gonna do: you take this piece of paper and this pen and you write it down. You write me a letter telling me exactly how you feel. Write down all your adolescent anger and rage, write down what you think of me and where you wish I would go. Then you bring it to me, folded once, and you put it in my hands. Without saying a word. And then you go and it's over.

Years later, when I die, you'll find a box in my study. Inside will be all the angry letters to me that I made you write. They'll be sealed in envelopes in chronological order, the date on which they were written labelled on the front.

Then, if you wish, you can revisit all the ridiculous and stupid arguments we almost had, the petty, childish squabbles and concerns, so world-consuming to your young mind then, so trivial and small now.

And in the last envelope will be a short note letting you know that I never read any of them.

LESSON 12
SPEAK YOUR MIND

LESSON

13

DONE

My mom loved her grandfather very much. He'd take her and her siblings for walks to the park or to the shops for sweets or to the restaurant to visit their father while he worked. He even bought her a bicycle one year for Christmas, one of her most treasured possessions.

Years later when she was an adult, long after he had passed, her mother told her the truth. Her parents bought her the bicycle, not her grandfather. He didn't like her. When she was born, her dad became deathly ill. Being a superstitious type, her grandfather blamed her for making her father sick. Even though her father eventually recovered, her grandfather resented her for nearly killing him for the rest of his days.

I don't know why her mother told my mom this. My mom used to say she wished she'd never found out. She'd much rather have preferred to have never known, to have kept her memory of her beloved grandfather and his wonderful gift intact.

My kids love their Nana, my wife's mother. She loves them, I'm pretty sure, but she doesn't buy them any gifts. She doesn't believe in buying toys for children, she didn't even for her own kids. She's also very cheap and extremely self-centred. But she loves her grandkids and they love her, so we buy them presents and tell them they're from her.

My wife and I have already decided that they must never know. Because as much as I hate the old battle-axe, my kids love her and she loves them.

But boy, does she ever have terrible taste in presents.

LESSON 13

IF YOU WANT SOMETHING DONE RIGHT, DO IT YOURSELF

LESSON

14

DREAM

T hat?
That, my friend, is a Clairtone Project G stereophonic high-fidelity sound system.

Manufactured in Rexdale, Ontario in 1964 by the Clairtone Sound Corporation, its stunning space-age styling and state-of-the-art electronics earned it design awards and universal accolades. Its four-foot tapered rosewood cabinet and massive globe speakers on each end made it almost seven feet long, so it's not for everybody. It's also a piece of furniture, not so subtly commanding a room. It was meant for trendsetters and swinging bachelor pads. It looked nothing like any other stereo system then or now. It became the epitome of sixties cool, featured in magazines and numerous Hollywood movies like *The Graduate*. Frank Sinatra and Hugh Hefner both owned one. Oscar Peterson praised its sound.

It was my dad's dream stereo system.

It took a year or so, but he finally got his. He had to go to a special convention and order it in. He must have been ecstatic when they delivered that bad boy to the house.

My mother kept it after he died. To her, it was just a working stereo. To us kids, it was more like a toy. We'd spend hours with it, watching LPs drop from the automatic turntable, putting our ears right up to the huge globe speakers, or just playing with the sliding roll-top door. We were the hippest kids in the neighbourhood and didn't even know it.

It's a little damaged now — my mother had it in direct sunlight for a while, so the wood is faded on one side. The speakers got dented a few times over the years. The radio works, but one of the speakers keeps cutting out, a common problem with these systems. And the holding tab for the turntable got lost in the move.

I don't use it anymore. It sits in my office, collecting dust and taking up space.

It's supposedly worth some money. I could sell it, heaven knows I could use the cash, but I don't know if I can.

It was my dad's dream stereo system. I feel like I have to honour that.

A dream that he had that was fulfilled. Maybe that's what it represents to me — hope. That you can have a dream and make it come true. How can you sell that? Exchange that for mere anonymous printed slips of paper?

I can't, so there it stays, emanating hope from its speakers instead of music, commanding my office, impressing an audience of one.

I just wish it didn't take up so much damn room.

LESSON 14
DREAM BIG

LESSON

15

LIVE

C hinese people are extremely superstitious. We're just not as superstitious as I thought we were.

I learned almost everything I know about Chinese culture from my mom and we both learned from my grandmother. Besides swear words, that included many, *many* superstitions.

For example, the number '4' is considered unlucky because the Chinese word for it sounds similar to the word for 'death'. Conversely, the number '8' is considered lucky because it sounds like the word for 'wealth'.

Red and pink are lucky colours. Oranges are always a good gift. You give money on Chinese New Year, you don't leave your chopsticks sticking out of your food, and owls are a bad omen.

Except that they're not.

My grandmother simply didn't like owls. They probably freaked her out with their big eyes, swivelling heads, and spooky noises. So to keep her life relatively owl-free, she told my mom, who later told me, that they were bad luck.

I only realized this recently. My wife, who is not Chinese, was talking to a Chinese friend and the topic of superstitions came up. My wife mentioned owls and her friend said that's not a

Chinese belief. Big surprise to me, but some quick checking revealed she's right.

In retrospect, I really should have figured this out earlier. My grandmother is the same person who told me that if a woman looks at a monkey while she's pregnant, her baby will look like a monkey. If you sit on a cushion that's still warm from somebody else sitting on it, you'll get a hemorrhoid. And a homosexual is someone who murders somebody, but we think she just got that word confused with 'homicidal'.

So now it means that I have to question everything I know — thought I knew — about Chinese people and Chinese culture. What's an actual Chinese superstition? What's an actual Chinese fact? What's merely my grandmother's irrational fear, or prejudice, or ignorance? Or my mother's?

Thinking back, I remember my mom telling me things were bad luck all the time, especially when she didn't want me doing them. I wasn't overly superstitious, but I heeded her warnings anyway. Wouldn't want to anger the gods — or karma or kismet, whatever. Besides, I needed all the luck I could get.

But now, I see what an excellent control technique it was. I never questioned their claims, I simply had no other source of information. I wasn't being made to obey them, I was placating our ancestors or tipping the cosmic balance in my favour. Everything I know could be wrong, but I'm not angry because of the sheer dumb brilliance of it all.

My kids are still pretty small, but there's already so much defiance in their eyes, in their actions. I'm going to want to control them a bit, both for their safety and my sanity. Do I lie to them and fill their heads with garbage, hoping they figure it out later (but sooner than I did)? There's precedence — Santa Claus, the Easter Bunny, etc. — except my kids' perceptions of their Chinese heritage hangs in the balance.

I'm leaning towards no. It's too important.

They need to learn about all the wonderful things their ancestors did and accomplished and created and built and believed. They need to be aware of Chinese culture and traditions and our contributions to the world. They're half-

Chinese — they should know what that means.
  I just wish I knew what to tell them.

LESSON 15

TO BELIEVE IN SOMETHING, AND NOT TO LIVE IT, IS DISHONEST

LESSON
16

TREATS

Hey Donny, I thought of you today.

You haven't crossed my mind in over thirty years, not since around the last time I ever saw you.

You lived a few streets over, I never knew exactly where. You'd drop by every once in a while to hang out. Our street was quieter, the kids were a bit gentler — I think you might have liked that.

Maybe your name was Danny...

You were a few years younger and small for your age. A cute little guy, endlessly charming. My mom was quite taken with you. Sometimes you wouldn't even play with us kids, you'd just sit on the retaining wall, talking to my mother for hours.

You were a foster kid. I didn't know what that was, so I asked my mom. You didn't talk about it and we didn't ask, so we never knew your exact circumstances. You always seemed happy and we liked you, so it wasn't all that important to us.

Or was it Jimmy?

One day, my mom gave all the neighbourhood kids a treat, an ice cream sandwich each. Everybody thanked her, but you were just blown away. Nobody ever saw such a grateful child. You thanked my mom over and over, beaming with pride and excitement, showing off your prize to all the others. We all had one of our own and we were used to kindness, so your reaction was a bit amusing. After a few bites, you raced off for home to show your foster mother.

Johnny? Tommy? Timmy?

You were back in ten minutes, dragged all the way by the ear by your foster mom. She pounded on our door, demanding to know if my mother had in fact given you an ice cream sandwich. My mom said yes, she had. She'd given all the kids one, not thinking it was a big deal. But your foster mother thought you'd stolen it. When my mom assured her you hadn't, she wanted to know why. Why would she do that? Why would anybody give something nice to a lying, thieving, no-good, piece-of-shit kid like…

Mikey. Your name was Mikey.

My mom came back into the house, shaking her head in disbelief. Your foster mom left and walked home, shaking her head in disbelief. You followed a few steps behind, head down, red-eared, the highs and lows of childhood melted out on your hands through a thin paper wrapper.

You only showed up once more after that. You sat on the wall and talked to my mom about something and then you were gone, quickly shifting into faded memory, then out of it completely until today. I don't know why I suddenly thought of you again after all these years, but I thought about you all day.

I wondered if you made it, if you were able to overcome such a stacked deck against you. I wondered if you got out of there and found something better, someplace where kindness wasn't such a rarity. I wondered if you grew up and had a family of your own, if you made a good father. I wondered if that small act showed you things could be different, that nice things could happen, or if it was a cruel tease, a quick glimpse of a life that remained out of reach, just a few streets over. I wondered if you'd like to be remembered or if you'd prefer that part of your life stayed where it was.

Then I got to thinking about all the kids from the old neighbourhood, who made it and who didn't and if there were any signs at the time — if we'd only known what to look for. Darren became a corporate banker, like his father, and races cars on the weekend. Mac lost his wife to his best friend, so he moved to Atlanta where he designs submarines. Steven and Stuart opened a small chain of restaurants together. Craig died in a head-on collision with an SUV. Laurel got pregnant early, married, and divorced, but her second marriage is better. I don't know what happened to Bobby, only that he was very unhappy. Nobody knows where Richard is, since he just kind of disappeared, but he's probably all right.

And then there's me. I drifted for a while, but now I have a crummy job, a house, and a mortgage as well as an amazing kid and a wonderful, beautiful, patient wife who would completely understand why I suddenly filled the freezer with ice cream sandwiches today, if only I could find the words to explain.

LESSON 16

No treats before dinner

LESSON
17

Tomorrow

When my wife and I first started dating, and then when we got married, we always ate in front of the TV. Just about every meal that we had at home, we'd pick a show, get dinner ready, then plant ourselves in front of the TV to watch and eat.

Then, when our first child was born, we stopped. We both agreed: we didn't want our kids to grow up like that. Dinnertime was family time, a chance to catch up with each other on the day's events, share an interesting story, connect.

It's something I think we'll continue doing. I remember as a kid, we never ate in front of the TV except snacks or a very special occasion. Saturdays when my grandmother was over were the best — sometimes we'd sit in the kitchen for two or three hours, just eating and talking and laughing.

I guess it all fell away when we grew up and moved out. Living on your own, sitting by yourself at the dinner table is kind of sad, so you turn on the TV just to have another voice in the room. The meals aren't so elaborate and only take as long to eat as the show lasts.

I like our little tradition. I like our mealtimes together. I know that it won't last forever, that our kids will grow up and move out, then it'll just be me and the wife. I wonder if the TV will go back on then.

Part of me wants this to last as long as possible. And part of me hopes my kids carry on the tradition with their families.

And the rest of me hopes I live long enough to catch up on all my shows.

LESSON 17

NEVER LEAVE THAT 'TIL TOMORROW WHICH YOU CAN DO TODAY

LESSON

18

CHILDREN

I always found people with kids to be extremely annoying, especially the ones who think everybody else should have kids too. The lines you always hear are "they've taught me so much" and "you can't really understand until you have kids of your own." And like so many other singles, I scoffed and sneered at the dumb breeders who were so stupid that they were being schooled by their children.

Now that I have children, I'm sorry to report that they were right on both counts. Your kids are not literally sitting you down for an instructional lesson, they provide insight into yourself through your actions and reactions.

For example, I've learned that I have a lot of weak spots. I've never taken so many shots to the genital area in my life. My kids' fingers seem to spend an inordinate amount of time in my eyes, nose, and mouth. And those tiny little elbows and knees are actually a lot sharper than they look.

I've learned that I have a high tolerance for messes and stickiness. I've learned to be more careful where I step. And I've learned how to fall asleep anywhere, anytime.

I've only now realized that you can never be too safe or too careful. Adult conversations are something to be savoured.

Residential speed limits are too fast and anything that can't be broken will simply be lost.

I've learned that my priorities were all wrong. I've learned that none of my concerns or needs are anywhere near as important as I thought they were. I've learned about self-sacrifice, how it feels to be truly vulnerable, that there are things in this world that matter more than I do, and that I have a seemingly endless capacity for love.

If you have kids of your own, then I'm not telling you anything you don't already know. If you don't have kids, then you can't really understand. Either way, I'm not going to say any more on the subject. And I hope you don't either, because I still find it extremely annoying since now I already know exactly what you're talking about.

LESSON 18

HE THAT HATH NO CHILDREN
DOTH BRING THEM UP WELL

19

ROOM

Years ago, I bought a hamster wheel. Then, my wife found it and made me throw it away.

"Did you used to have a hamster?" she asked.
"No. It was in case I ever got one."
"Do you want one?"
"No."
"Then why do you have a hamster wheel?"
"I told you: it's for if I ever need it."

Here comes the shouting.

"Why would you buy something you don't need?!?"
"So that if I do need it, I don't have to run out and buy one!"
"But you're not going to get a hamster! You don't want one!"
"I can't predict the future! I can only prepare for it!"
"What is wrong with you?!?"
"Nothing! And I have a hamster wheel!"

So... now I *don't* have a hamster wheel. Turns out, they don't work very well if they get stepped on a few times.

To date, I still do not have, and have never had, a hamster. It's okay, I never really wanted one. I had a hamster wheel once and that was enough.

LESSON 19
CLEAN YOUR ROOM

20

Do

G od, I hate the park.

I'm not doing anything. I'm just standing around, watching my kid play. Of all the useless non-activities I have to do every damn weekend, this has to be the most stultifyingly boring and non-productive.

I have things to do. I work all week, then I have to spend my time off doing this? Nothing? I can't even look at my phone or the other parents will silently disapprove and think I'm a dick. Heaven forbid my kid befriends one of theirs and we end up having to spend time together. Is there even a name for that tenuous social relationship? No, of course not. Why would you name something you wished didn't exist?

Yes, I see you on the slide. Is that why I'm here? To watch you do stuff? I guess I'm supposed to be keeping you safe. How long does that last? How old is old enough to take care of yourself? When can you go to the park on your own?

When do I get my life back? It's not just the park. It's like every aspect of my life, every minute of the day has been turned over to you. Yes, that's a great drawing of some stick figures, just like the one you did five minutes ago. You can count to ten? Great. I've been doing it for years. How to tie your shoes? I don't really give it any thought, perhaps you're overanalyzing it.

I guess I'm supposed to be nurturing you, teaching you all the things you don't know. Which is everything. You're a blank slate, an empty vessel, and I'm expected to fill that with all my accumulated wisdom and knowledge. Seriously, isn't there a book you could read? After I teach you how to read, of course.

Who taught me to read? Can't we get that person to teach you? Who taught me everything? Crap. I'm stuck doing this forever, aren't I? Wasting my time on you... I mean, investing my time in you. You don't even have homework yet. That's going to be a whole other nightmare. Years to go, then you're off to college. Then does it end? Or will you be phoning home to ask me even more stuff — adult stuff?

Why couldn't you have been born fully formed? This is painful. Why don't you know everything you need to know? How is this advantageous evolutionarily? Why don't...

What? No, I don't know how to transform your little robot toy. Oh, like that? How did you...?

Don't you dare roll your eyes at me, mister. You think that's funny? How many books have you read? *Without* pictures? Yeah, I didn't think so. You want to run some times tables next? Oh, what are those, you say?

You think you're so smart? You've got nothing on your old man! I'm years ahead of you! I know a million things you don't!

And you know what? I'm going to teach them to you. Partly because I should and partly to rub your nose in it. Look, here's another thing your dad knows and you don't! And another thing! And *another!*

I've only got a few more years to feel smarter than you. Gotta take advantage of this while I can.

Come on. Let's go back to the park, where there's nothing to learn.

LESSON 20

THOSE WHO CAN, DO.
THOSE WHO CAN'T, TEACH.

LESSON

21

IMITATION

I swear a bit too much in front of my kids. My wife is not happy about it and voices her displeasure often. But I can see that it gives my son a little thrill.

I can't help myself. The curse words just come out. When I hurt myself, when I'm frustrated or angry, I revert to the way I always acted, the way I always talked before I had kids, which was a long time.

That said, I don't believe a little bad language is an entirely negative thing.

My son knows better than to swear — he'll get in trouble. At school, with his mom, even with me. I'm a hypocrite. But he does enjoy it when I do it.

I guess, for him, it's a little peek into the adult world. Here's yet another thing that grown-ups do that you're not allowed to, though you get to listen in on occasion. Other things will come along and intrigue you, like smoking and drinking and drugs, hopefully not for a long time and hopefully in moderation, if at all.

I don't believe overhearing a bit of swearing is bad for kids. You don't want to make something too taboo or it becomes all the more mystifying and enticing, the forbidden fruit. And we all know how that ended.

I'll probably give him his first drink, a sip of something, so he can see what it's about with me around, instead of going crazy at a house party with a bunch of strangers somewhere. His grandmother smokes, maybe he can try a puff there. Not sure what to do about the drugs, but I have some time to figure something out.

I'm not completely sure if I'm right, but that's what I believe. If Dad does it, then it can't be all that cool and mysterious.

I hope I'm right. I mean, I *fucking* hope I'm right.

LESSON 21

IMITATION IS THE SINCEREST FORM OF FLATTERY

LESSON

22

PROUD

I'm actually looking forward to being an embarrassment to my kids. Right now, I'm Cool Dad, but when they get to public school and the peer pressure kicks in, I'm going to be all over that. Once I detect they can feel shame, Dork Dad will take over.

I'll pull up in the schoolyard in my beater car, wearing my ratty old clothes, blaring my hopelessly outdated music. I'll call out to them as loudly as possible, maybe do a little dance while I wait for them to trudge towards me, then try to give them great big hugs while they roll their eyes as high and as far back in their heads as possible.

I won't even be consistent, either. Bad jokes, funny voices, singing to the radio, or awkwardly trying to be one of the guys — keep 'em guessing, on their toes.

Truly, it's the role I was born to play. I never was cool, not ever. I tried, but it never worked out. It just wasn't me.

I really think I'll be good at it. After all, I've had lots of practice. I've been an embarrassment to my mother for as long as I can remember.

LESSON 22

BE PROUD OF WHERE YOU COME FROM

23

JUDGE

I have a photograph of my father with his brother. You wouldn't even know they were related.

My father was tall, handsome, and broad-shouldered. My uncle was also tall, but he's hunched over, so he looks much smaller.

My father is standing with his feet firmly planted, back straight, looking right at the camera. My uncle is leaning up against a chair, looking sideways through half-closed eyes.

My father worked hard his whole life and sent money to his brother so he could immigrate to Canada. My uncle gambled and partied the money away.

My father put himself through business school, then started his own successful company. My uncle cut fish in a plant.

My father had a black belt in kung fu. My uncle smoked and drank until he got cirrhosis.

In the photo, my father exudes confidence and strength. My uncle looks like a lizard that's come out to sun itself on a rock.

My father was humble and never bragged about himself. My uncle liked to act like a big shot to try to impress me.

But how could he? I had the photograph.

When I tell my son to watch his posture, to stand up straight and not slouch, this is what I'm thinking about. Of the two brothers, which one do you want to look like? Which one would you rather be?

My father was killed when he was just 31 years old. My uncle lived into his seventies, eventually dying of that cirrhosis.

After all these years, the answer has never wavered. Even if my own accomplishments didn't compare, even if my own achievements weren't so grand, at least I looked the part.

LESSON 23
DON'T JUDGE A BOOK BY ITS COVER

LESSON
24

NICE

There was this girl I knew. She was beautiful and sexy and amazing, and she used to flirt with me so I figured she was interested in me. I was definitely interested in her. But every time I saw her, my heart would jump in my throat, and my stomach would turn over, and I'd start to sweat and tingle, and my knees would wobble, and my throat would tighten, and I'd lose my words.

So I never even asked her out.

Then I met a girl and I was comfortable with her right away. We put each other at ease and we got along really well, so I married her and we had you.

And while we continue to get along, you can probably guess that I think about the other girl constantly. What if I'd asked her out? What if I'd married her? After all these years, would I still jump at the sight of her? Would I still have the same feelings, the ones I've never had with your mother?

It's useless to keep asking myself the same questions over and over. I can't change what happened. I can't go back in time and tell myself to ask her out, to find out or live a lifetime of horrible regret, complacency, and surrender.

But I can warn you. I can try to convince you that you have to take those chances. When you meet that girl that intrigues you, scares you, overwhelms you, you have to get over that stupid fear and at least try. If you need convincing, just look at me, your possible future. Self-loathing, regretful, stupid, unloving me...

Oh, fuck, like, don't tell your mom, okay? She doesn't deserve that. I do love her, it's just not what it should be, not what it could have been. We still get along, we work well together, we're... comfortable.

It's just... I'm sure she has her regrets too and I'm pretty sure I'm one of them. But she can't change anything either or she would, and I would, and then you'd be pretty fucked, wouldn't you?

LESSON 24

IF YOU CAN'T SAY SOMETHIN' NICE, DON'T SAY NOTHIN' AT ALL

25

WEIRD

Everybody thinks they're normal. Everybody thinks that everyone else had the same childhood that they had, their parents treated them the same as other parents treated their kids, and their experiences were the same as everybody else.

Then you get out in the world, you meet other former kids, and inconsistencies start to appear. You might have suspected earlier, when you were a kid and you didn't like going over to a friend's house because his dad was 'weird', but it doesn't really become evident until you're an adult and you start comparing notes with other adults.

Some kids have great parents, some have terrible parents, some have siblings, some don't. Some kids grow up in big cities, but there are small towns and farming communities too. Some kids even grow up in other countries, believe it or not. Rich or poor, popular or lonely, spoiled or neglected, loved or not-so-loved, there are so many different variables to make up a life, yet we all think that we're the normal one.

I had an inkling that there was something different about the school I went to from grades 2 through 6, but I could never figure out what. I'd describe parts of it to my high school classmates, but they'd laugh at me in disbelief, so I stopped talking about it. But I'd hear about their experiences and wonder why I never did that, or why they did things so differently, or why I was taught subjects that they weren't and vice-versa. But then, thinking I was the normal one, I figured that they must have been the ones missing out somehow.

Then, one day, as an adult, while researching something in the main city library, I came across a book that I recognized. It was a book espousing the philosophies of the grade school that I had gone to. The founder had written many books on education, early learning, and child development and here they were on the shelf in front of me in the real world.

"I remember this one. I've seen this one at the school. We actually had this one. And this one... What section of the library am I in?"

I looked up at the sign above my head. 'Occult'.

"Oh, wow," I thought to myself, "that makes so much more sense."

LESSON 25

IT'S WEIRD NOT TO BE WEIRD

LESSON

26

SECRETS

My grandmother on my mother's side told the most horrible stories. She grew up a Chinese woman in Canada in the 1920s, so it wasn't going to be an easy life. Racism, child abuse, starvation, torture — this is what we grew up with. Or, rather, she did — we just grew up with the stories, constant reminders of how lucky we were.

I loved my grandmother, but when I think of her, I think of her sitting in the kitchen with that hollow, faraway look in her eyes, telling us the horrible stories over and over again. Getting chased home, being called names, having rocks thrown at her, the cruel, sadistic woman who was supposed to care for her after her mother died, the whippings, the beatings, getting tied to a stake outside and doused with water in the middle of winter as punishment...

Perhaps the worst part isn't that I think she was holding back — she never mentioned sexual abuse, but I could guess that it happened. Perhaps the worst part is that she told us these stories so many times, we stopped listening.

We'd laugh them off, even right in front of her.

"Oh, she's telling that story again. Yes, we know what happened, you've told us a thousand times."

Then we'd try to change the subject, but she'd keep dragging it back.

"Don't you have any *happy* stories?" we'd implore.

"No, nothing good ever happened to me."

When she got sick for the last time, she had a prolonged hospital stay. The nurses there all loved her.

"Oh, she tells the most wonderful stories!" they'd say.

"What the hell are you talking about? What stories?"

"About visiting China and seeing tea ceremonies and travelling and..."

"How come we've never heard these stories?" we demanded.

"Not for you. Only good stuff for other people. Bad stuff for family only."

"Gee, thanks. Why couldn't we have gotten some of the good stuff?"

"What good stuff? Nothing good ever happened to me."

She was kind of demented by then. Too late to get the good stuff.

As my mother gets older, she tends to get fixated on the negative things that have happened to her in her life. She's starting to repeat stories that we've heard over and over with some amount of regret mixed in. Racism, sexism, missed opportunities, but there was no abuse — my grandmother was a kind woman and she married a kind man.

When my mind starts to wander, I think of the people who were mean to me, who wronged me, who screwed me over. But again, no abuse. Just like my sister, my cousins, my aunts and uncles, my nieces and nephews, and, of course, my kids. There were a few iffy boyfriends along the way, but they got sent packing ages ago. We all heard the stories enough times that something's going to stick, whether you're listening or not.

So maybe my grandmother's horrible stories did serve their purpose. I wish she'd had a happier, less painful life. But her legacy is staggeringly beautiful, just like my memory of her sitting at our kitchen table, horrible stories and all.

LESSON 26

KEEP YOUR SECRETS SAFE

27

RAINBOW

I'm the fun parent! I'm in charge of games, I buy the toys, I conjure laughs out of nowhere! I'll sit and play with you for hours, I do funny voices at storytime, and nobody's better at finding your tickle spots!

Mommy is the serious parent. She doesn't goof around like Daddy does. She doesn't tell very good jokes. She never liked toys, not even when she was a kid. She tries, but it doesn't seem easy for her. Not like Daddy!

When they fall and hurt themselves, when the tears are coming, or if they just need a hug, they'll take Daddy if Mommy isn't there. But if she is, it's Mommy every time.

Mommy kisses the boo-boos, she dries the tears, she knows what to say to make the bad feelings go away. She comforts them when they're sick, she's the one they call for at night when the dark is too much, and apparently she gives the best hugs. Mommy is the clear favourite, when it counts.

I'm the fun parent. But it's not always fun.

LESSON 27

IF YOU WANT THE RAINBOW,
YOU GOTTA PUT UP WITH THE RAIN

28

ROLLING

I used to live here, but I had to move away. Too many ghosts. This exact spot is where a friendship ended, that's where she broke my heart. I wasted so much time over here, I failed over there.

There were good times too, but as the city changed and people moved away, everything faded into melancholia and loneliness. No new memories were forming, experiences weren't happening.

The new city held promise, but it quickly wore me down. New locations, new acquaintances signalled hope, but with added responsibilities and without the vitality of youth, resentment grew and covered everything with dust, made me feel even older, more unwanted.

Coming back to visit my mom, I barely recognize the place. I know I can't stay, just long enough to remember a few things and register regret.

Another new city, but this one will be different. This is the one where my kids will grow up. This is the city where they'll make friends and start to explore the world, go to school and learn to drive, get kissed and get drunk, and experience life for the first time.

Then they'll move away, but I'll stay here, holding a spot for them for when they come to visit. I'll try my best to keep their memories safe, but I wasn't even able to do that for myself.

I should probably try to get out to see my mom sometime. She thinks I've been avoiding her.

LESSON 28
A ROLLING STONE GATHERS NO MOSS

LESSON
29

IMPORTANT

Whenever I run into friends I haven't seen in a while, I can't help but notice that they're getting old.

Some have gained weight. Some have lost hair. A good number have gotten married and had kids.

Just about all of them have settled down into boring, unimaginative lives. Except for one...

I won't say his name, just that he's a well-practiced liar. Every time we meet, he tells me how wonderful his life is going. Maybe his job is so fantastic and he's making great money. Or he got bored with that and went back to school. Or he's publishing yet another magazine.

Whatever. I know none of it is true, but I smile and nod and congratulate him because I know that's what he wants. We've been friends for a long time.

I ran into him just a few weeks ago. And he looks great.

LESSON 29
IT'S NICE TO BE IMPORTANT,
BUT IT'S MORE IMPORTANT TO BE NICE

LESSON

30

WORDS

My uncle Jeffrey died and we did not mourn.
He was not a nice man.
He yelled
A lot.
At us
At his own kids
At his wife.
A lot.
More than we knew.
He was controlling and domineering
And greedy and selfish and demeaning
And he screamed until he got his way.
He told his kids what to do in every aspect of their lives.
He told his wife what to do so much
That it was easier to just go along with it
Than to endure the yelling
Which came anyway.
He lied.
He stole
From work

From strangers
From my grandmother.
You would have liked him.
He was very charming
If you didn't know him,
If he hadn't tried to take advantage of you yet.
He had a good job
But no money
Because he lost it all
On the stock market,
On bad land deals,
And useless product investments.
When we were younger,
Family gatherings were tense
Because we didn't know if he would get angry
Over something small.
When we got older,
Family gatherings were tense
Because nobody knew if this would be the time
I finally punched him out.
He cheated on his wife
And blamed her for it.
The other woman knew he was married.
We weren't angry at her,
We just felt pity.
When he finally left my aunt, it was to her great relief
But with crippling debt.
When he died,
His new wife came to Canada
And couldn't figure out why nobody was sad.
My kids are too young,
They will never meet him.
That's all right,
One less thing to explain.
Over the years,

We forgave him
Repeatedly
Not because he was family,
Not because my aunt chose to stay with him,
But because
Once,
A long time ago,
He identified my father's body
So my mother wouldn't have to.

LESSON 30

ACTIONS SPEAK LOUDER THAN WORDS

LESSON
31

GOLD

E very few years, I buy a box of Twinkies. And every time, I'm disappointed by how terrible they are.

I used to love Twinkies. Nothing would rev me up like seeing that familiar box in the groceries Mom brought home. Maybe they weren't a major part of my childhood, but they certainly were a highlight.

I just can't believe, refuse to believe, that I don't like them anymore. Maybe I had lower standards back then. Maybe they changed the recipe. Or maybe I've changed. Maybe I've changed so much that I don't even recognize an old friend.

I know that's a lot of baggage for a stupid spongecake, but I need to know if my childhood wasn't as good as I thought it was.

Hey kids, here you go. Daddy still doesn't like Twinkies again. Somebody might as well enjoy them, while they can.

LESSON 31
NOTHING GOLD CAN STAY

LESSON

32

WATCH

I've lightly toyed with the idea of opening a store. The catch would be, I'd only sell stuff that I'd found.

Since I was a kid, my mom always told me to keep an eye on the ground because you can find money that people have dropped. So I did and she was right. I've found lots of coins over the years, from pennies to quarters to commemorative silver dollars, new and old and even from other countries. I've spotted dollar bills from moving cars, crumpled up and swept into corners or just laying out on the street for anybody to find if they're looking down.

I've found other things, too. Shopping lists, toys, playing cards, pens, photographs, letters, clothing, jewellery, books, keys, ID badges, and once, a live fish. Some of it I kept, most I left where I found it. The fish was delicious.

By looking down all the time, I'm sure I've missed things, though. Sunsets, rare birds, cute girls trying to make eye contact... But then, on those times when I did look up, who knows what I didn't see on the ground? I'll never know.

I'm not sure what to tell my kids to do. I don't want them to miss out on things like I probably did, but then, finding money is pretty awesome. That's a great view there, but you've stepped in dog poop. Maybe I won't tell them one way or the other and just let them find out for themselves, resigning myself to cleaning their shoes really well in the meantime.

But back to the store — I don't know if it would be such a good business plan. All the stuff I've found would make an eclectic, unreliable inventory that could have easily ended up in someone else's possessions if they'd only been more attentive. I'm not even sure I'd want to go check out a store that only sold things I'd found, let alone a store that only sold things that somebody else found.

But I tell you, I'd be beating down the door to get to a store that only sold things I'd lost.

LESSON 32
WATCH YOUR STEP

LESSON
33

ROCK

We were driving to my school, but I wasn't going to class. Mom was going to vote in something called an 'election', so I was excited.

The parking lot was fuller than usual, with a steady stream of people entering and leaving the front door. Signs had been posted directing everybody to the gym. No dodgeball today, it had been transformed into — well, not something magical, but definitely different than I had seen before. Tables ringed the outer edges and curtained booths stood mysteriously at strategic locations. I eyed them cautiously — she hadn't mentioned those. People were disappearing inside for a few minutes, then re-emerging and either quickly leaving or hanging around to talk to someone they knew.

I looked around for any familiar faces, but saw only adults. Okay, so there wouldn't be any fun, but I got to see my school gym dressed up as something else. Totally worth being dragged along.

A man crossed my mom's name off a list. She had already told me I wasn't old enough, that I couldn't vote until an inconceivable number of years had gone by — I was fine with that, I was used to it. I was just happy to be there as if that was somehow part of the process.

She told me to wait, not to move, as she swept behind the curtain. I stood transfixed, waiting for some transformation, an exultation, a revelatory flash of illumination. I had seen something like this in movies, but a costumed superhero emerged and flew up into the heavens, not my mom in her regular jacket simply saying, "All done, let's go."

Back in the car, I pressed her for details. Who was that man you talked to? What was it like inside the booth? How old do I have to be again? Will the gym still be like that tomorrow? Who did you vote for?

"I don't have to tell you."

I had seen the candidates' names. They meant absolutely nothing to me. I didn't know their platforms, their politics, what they stood for, or their intentions. I didn't even know what they were running for. I just wanted to know who my mom had picked.

"It's a secret ballot. That means my vote is a secret. I don't have to tell anybody."

"Not even me?"

"Not even you."

The betrayal stung deeper than anything I had ever experienced. What was this 'democracy' that could turn my own mother against me?

I lost my desire to vote.

Still haven't found it.

LESSON 33
ROCK THE BOAT

34

INVOLVED

Apparently, after three beers, I'm a terrible father.

Lips are loosened as inhibitions fall away, things that would not normally be said are said. Unnecessary things. Hurtful things. Perhaps true, perhaps not.

After the third beer, on the way to six, that's when it starts getting ugly. Alcohol isn't just a coping mechanism, you can go on the offensive with it, too.

I see the sideways glances around the room, the looks of resignation, the attempts to shrink away, to vanish. The criticisms flow more freely after beer number four, number five. This is how the evening is going to be, just like yesterday and the day before and tomorrow and the day after that.

There's nothing I can do about it. Alcoholism is a sickness. It grips your brain, your body, it contorts and distorts, it angers and saddens and gives you an excuse. Not that you need one, you won't remember anything in the morning anyway.

But *they* will. They're going to remember for a long time. You could see it in their eyes if you could focus yours.

They might even take after dear old Dad and start drinking as soon as they come in the door after work, not stopping until bedtime. Or maybe they'll be so disgusted they'll never touch a drop. It's so hard to know how things are going to turn out.

My kids are older now, old enough to have questions, and I'm not sure if I have answers. No one in my family ever drank. Get-togethers and holiday gatherings were relatively stress-free affairs without some ticking timebomb sitting in the corner, not like now. I just don't have the experience nor the skills to even know how to deal with this.

I don't give a damn what you say, I'm a good father. And it's none of your fucking business how I raise my kids. Just like it's none of my fucking business that you drink way too much while you're raising yours.

In the car on the way home, my son asks why his uncle said those things to me. I tell him it's because he's an alcoholic and I explain what that is. I ask him if he agrees with his uncle, does he think I'm a bad father? My son says no.

I thank him and tell him he's a good kid and I love him. And his uncle loves him and loves his own kids, despite anything he might say.

Then we drive the rest of the way home in silence, because there's nothing else I can explain.

LESSON 34
GET INVOLVED

LESSON

35

LEARN

My mom never trusted my judgment. I don't know why she ever asked me my opinion or how to do anything. Every time it was the same thing: I would tell her my answer, she would immediately say I was wrong, she'd ask somebody else, usually my sister, then she'd tell me what the other person said, I'd tell her that it was the exact same thing I'd said, and she'd say no, it wasn't. Frustrating, to be sure, and she could never tell me why she did it.

Now I have kids of my own and I'm doing the same thing. They're not stupid, they're actually quite bright, but they don't know anything because they're still just little kids.

I suppose after a decade or so of constantly correcting them (learning opportunities!) and second-guessing them, it could become so ingrained in me that I won't be able to stop. I may never see informed, intelligent, reasonable adults capable of making their own decisions and solving their own problems, just ignorant little kids fumbling about, forever needing somebody older and more knowledgeable to guide and correct them.

Then I look in the mirror and wonder if I'll ever see it there, either.

I still hope I will and I also hope I can change and treat my children differently so they don't grow up with the same crushing self-doubt giving way to frustration and exasperation as I did.

But you know, always having to correct them — it's awfully good for my self-confidence. Makes me feel really smart and stuff. Who knows, time comes, I may not want to give it up.

You may disagree, but why would I trust your judgment?

LESSON 35
YOU'RE NEVER TOO OLD TO LEARN SOMETHING NEW

LESSON

36

TEACH

I struggled with Obsessive-Compulsive Disorder for years, so I'm always on the lookout for signs of it in my kids.

I know what to look for, but it's entirely possible I read too much into things. If they line their toys up a little too carefully, if they won't step on any cracks, if they're washing their hands a bit too long, or if they won't colour outside the lines, I have to step in.

Come on, kids! Don't worry about the mess, we can go around it! They're just books, a few creased pages are fine! They're dry cracker crumbs, we'll clean it up later! Oops, I 'accidentally' knocked over your block tower, *ha ha*, sorry about that!

It's *killing* me. I'm going against one of my most basic natures to try to ensure my kids don't end up like me. If it works, great. If not, if they rebel, maybe they'll spend some extra time tidying things up.

Either way, I get something I want.

LESSON 36

YOU CAN'T TEACH AN OLD DOG NEW TRICKS

LESSON

37

FRIENDS

She wasn't particularly attractive. Not unattractive, mind you, just not outstanding. Not really the type of girl that usually interested me. And yet, I found myself irresistibly drawn to her. Not helplessly, hopelessly in love — I was merely compelled by her.

There were no fantasies at play, romantic, sexual, or other. She intrigued me. I knew next to nothing about her: we shared a chemistry class, we had no common friends, she always wore the same heavy coat, even in summer. But sometimes that's part of the draw — the less you know about somebody, the more appealing they are. There's still some mystery, the unknown — possibilities. It's when you get to know them that the flaws start to turn up. Takes you for granted, leaves the milk out, farts in her sleep — all the things that drive you away or bring you closer together. If I can overlook this minor quirk, I can overlook this egregious offence. Or not.

A good test of a relationship is if you can be bored together. It's not all beer-soaked hilarity and jumping on the bed in your underwear. There's also folding the laundry and hangover cures. If you can successfully kill an entire Sunday together, then maybe you can make it to fifty years.

But it never got that far. We never dated, or fell in love, or even talked to each other. The attraction confused me, so I never acted on it. And the opposite of action is inaction and nothing gets done and nothing happens. And life, such as it is, goes on. Somebody else takes you for granted, she farts in somebody else's bed.

Then one day, you're cleaning out a closet at your mother's house and you find a box of your old things. You pick up your childhood teddy bear and for some reason you think of a girl. And that's when you see the resemblance...

The sudden realization makes you laugh. And you never think of her again.

But you can't bring yourself to throw away the bear.

LESSON 37

OLD FRIENDS ARE BEST

LESSON
38

SAID

I tell my kids I love them pretty much every day. I don't remember my mother telling me that.

Not that she didn't love me, I'm sure she did. I just hated hearing it.

I probably reacted negatively whenever she tried to tell me. Enough times that she stopped saying she loved me. For long enough that I stopped believing it.

Or maybe I just took it for granted. I assumed she would always love me, no matter what I did, no matter how crappy I treated her. It didn't need to be said, it just was and always would be.

I'm not going to assume my kids think this. They're still young, they don't flinch and groan when I tell them I love them or give them hugs and kisses. I know it'll come when they get older, but I'm going to persevere. I can't let it go unsaid until it's too late and they don't believe it anymore. It's important to let them know how much I love them, no matter what.

So, yeah, turns out wives are like that too.

LESSON 38
LITTLE SAID IS SOONEST MENDED

LESSON
39

SEEN

If I could go back in time, obviously, I'd try to stop Hitler, but the other thing I'd like to do is try to save my dad.

I don't know all the rules of time travel, or if there even are any, but if I could go back as myself as I am now, it would be easy. I could just knock on the door, introduce myself, show my ID and photos from the future, point out the familial resemblance, then warn him about going in to work that day.

However, if I had to occupy my own body at that time, on that day, it could be a problem. At two and a half years old, my means of communication were somewhat limited.

I probably wasn't talking too much, or too coherently, if my own two-and-a-half-year-old is a good guideline. Writing would also be out, maybe even proper spelling if I had access to a typewriter or alphabet blocks. I don't know how time travel would affect the mind, I'm hoping at least I'd still remember why I was there.

No, I would have to resort to whatever a two-and-a-half-year-old me would be capable of doing — latching onto him as he tried to leave, screaming at him not to go, pleading as well as I could, for his sake, for mine, for my mom's.

So when my son does that to me, I have to pause at the door, look down at him right in his eyes, and try to tell if it's him or if it's future him come back to save me from an as yet unknown fate. Try to discern just how desperate he is, if he's trying to save my life or if he just doesn't want me to go to work so we can play all day.

Look out the window, check left, check right. Take a deep breath, open the door. And go.

LESSON 39

CHILDREN SHOULD BE SEEN AND NOT HEARD

LESSON

40

REWARD

My kids are home sick from school again. Nothing serious, probably just a 24-hour flu, so I'm not worried at all. In fact, I kind of enjoy it. They're asleep in their beds, the house is quiet, and luckily I wasn't working today, so I'm not losing money. But best of all, they need me.

They're getting so big and independent and so capable of doing things on their own, and eager to do so, it's getting rarer and rarer that they come to me for help. I remember how they'd cling to me when they were babies, so helpless and fearful, and how good it felt to be such a source of comfort. Now, it's almost like I'm in their way.

I should enjoy my growing independence, just as they enjoy theirs, but I can't help but feel a little sad. I wonder if this feeling will ever go away. I wonder if my mom feels it whenever I call her for advice and if I will when my kids are grown and they call me. I realize that this is how it's supposed to be and that if they ever need me again like they did when they were babies, then something has gone terribly, terribly wrong.

My daughter cries out. I give her some more medicine and a sip of water, then I sit with her, stroking her hair until she falls asleep again. She's miserable, but I can't help smiling.

I think of calling my mom, but decide against it. I'm a grown-up, I can handle this. On the one hand, there's the feeling of being needed, but on the other, there's the feeling of a job well done. I'll feel that someday too, I hope, but in the meantime, I can wait.

LESSON 40

THE REWARD OF A THING WELL DONE
IS TO HAVE DONE IT

LESSON
41

CHARACTER

I used to buy a new box of Q-Tips every 500 days. It wasn't a routine or anything special. The box holds 500 Q-Tips, I use one a day — 500 days.

Then I got married, and then we had a kid, and then another, and now our Q-Tip consumption is completely unpredictable. They're cleaning ears, they're cleaning around the tub, they're being used for art projects, heaven knows what else.

It's not a big deal. I still use one a day, so I can keep a pretty close eye on how many are left, then add it to the shopping list as needed.

But it's not a box every 500 days anymore.

There was a certainty to that, a comfort, a consistency that's lacking from my life right now. Everything's in tumult, everything's changing constantly, but that should be okay, too.

Children should learn how to adapt, to not get stuck in a routine of a rut, to embrace the chaos and try to control it and thrive in and off of it.

They do need some stability in their lives. We all do — I definitely include myself in that, but not to the point of stagnation. Roll with the punches, go with the flow, live for the now, that sort of thing.

And, also importantly, they should learn not to romanticize a box of fucking Q-Tips.

LESSON 41

CHARACTER IS HABIT LONG CONTINUED

LESSON

42

Sow

I could never figure out why these older women I had never met before hated me on sight.

Most people brag about their kids, whether it's warranted or not. They go on and on about what their kids are doing, what trophies or awards or achievements they've earned, how smart or athletic or talented they are — all the promise and accolades and recognition. These people are annoying.

Some people complain about their kids, whether it's warranted or not. Trouble at school, trouble with the law, disrespectful, rebellious, disobedient. These people are rarer — who wants to display their shame and parenting failures to everybody? — but they *are* more interesting to listen to.

Then there's my mom. If you talked to her about me, you'd think I was a serial killer. She made me sound like I was lighting fires in the basement when I needed a break from torturing puppies and knocking down old ladies.

I was an honour roll student who stayed in every weekend through high school. I was a nerd who didn't get invited to parties. I never smoked, drank, or did drugs. But my mom likes to complain. She liked the attention and the sympathy it got her, so she told all her friends I was the devil incarnate.

I only found out when I met one of her friends who, instead of just giving me the usual disapproving look, actually started berating me for something awful I hadn't done.

When I confronted my mom about it, she denied it at first, then told me she was justified because she thought I was lazy and played too many videogames. Perhaps I'm biased, but I didn't feel it was comparable.

So guess who won't be complaining about his kids? It's too early to tell what kind of trouble they'll get into, and when they do, why would I want to talk about that? I don't need the attention. Be they little cherubs or little hellions, it's none of your business. Sorry if that bores you.

But I don't hold it against my mom. Turns out, I didn't really care what a bunch of older women I didn't know thought about me. And I may not have been the worst son ever, but I wasn't the best, either.

And it's only fair — you should have heard what I said about her to my friends.

LESSON 42
As you sow, so shall you reap

LESSON

43

ORIGINALITY

I don't want to be one of those boring old farts who's always saying to his kids, "When I was your age..."

I compare my kids to myself all the time because I use my life as the baseline for what's normal, as we all do, so right there you know it has to be a faulty assumption.

But, putting that aside, I'm still not going to verbalize it to make my kids feel bad that they're not living up to the standard I set back in the day.

Things are different now. Society is different, schools are different — the media, our culture, the neighbourhood, our family, all these things have changed in countless ways. I can't hold my kids to a standard that just doesn't exist anymore.

They're going to have to find their own paths and set their own pace. They'll reach their milestones in their time and if it's before I did or after should be irrelevant. I'm not trying to best my kids, I'm trying to better them.

Also, I don't want them to realize just yet that, for all my early achievements, I didn't get too far. That'll come eventually and, when it does, I don't want to feel any worse than I do now that I didn't live up to the standard I set for myself.

The standard I set a long time ago, when I was their age.

LESSON 43

IT IS BETTER TO FAIL IN ORIGINALITY THAN TO SUCCEED IN IMITATION

LESSON
44

LOST

I used to stutter when I was a kid. Not all the time, and not too severely. Only when I got stressed or nervous or when too many people were paying attention to me. It didn't really hamper me, but it was embarrassing.

I stuttered into my twenties. Then somebody told me that they used to be really self-conscious until they realized that nobody cared if you looked stupid because they were all too worried about looking stupid themselves.

So I stopped caring about what other people thought of me. It was rather freeing, to say the least. I did what I wanted, I said what I wanted, and people did talk about me, but it didn't matter anymore. They didn't matter anymore, their opinions of me didn't matter, I was who I was and I wasn't going to be who they tried to mock me into being. And the stutter went away.

I definitely want my kids to come to this realization sooner than I did, but I wonder if I should tell them or not. All my efforts and advice on dealing with the world — am I giving them too many of the answers? Should they be finding out for themselves? After all, those are the best lessons, the ones you learn on your own from personal experience.

I watch my kids at school with other kids and feel some

apprehension. They hold back, they don't join in, they hide their faces, they don't speak up. And I watch the other kids, the ones who seem so fearless and independent — I wonder how they got to be that way, how their parents are raising them, and if they think I'm doing a crap job raising mine.

So I guess I got rid of the stutter, but the insecurities remained. Maybe it's because some helpful soul told me what to do, instead of me learning it on my own. But if that never happened, how would you ever learn anything?

If my kids stutter, I'll think I'll clue them in. I'll let them know that nobody's really paying attention to them, that they're all trying to not look stupid themselves, that nobody really cares what you look like or say or do.

The insecurities have to come from somewhere, don't they?

LESSON 44

HE WHO HESITATES IS LOST

LESSON
45

MATTER

Don't get me wrong, I love my kids, but I hate being a father. It's so much responsibility and they take up all my time. My schedule is so full now with playdates and appointments. And forget weekends. I can't do what I want or even what I need to do. I can't eat what I want because I have to make sure they'll eat it, too. I can't say what I want because I have to set an example. It's like I'm not *me* anymore.

On the other hand, I love being married, but I can't stand my wife. I was never any good at dating, so having a regular companion that has more than one evening invested in me is fantastic. I always have someone to talk to at dinner and plans for New Year's Eve. But she's so annoying. And a bit of a slob. She has terrible taste in movies, she never wants sex, and she's a fussier eater than the kids.

I didn't choose my kids. We chose to have them, but we didn't pick them out of a line or anything, we got what we got. And I love them to bits, unconditionally.

My wife — I chose her, flaws and all, and she makes me so unhappy. I screwed things up with the woman I wanted, so I settled for her. That was my choice and I made it even after much deliberation.

I look back at my life decisions and I see a pattern. Whenever I had to make a choice, I chose poorly and suffered for it. Relationships, education, employment opportunities — when the decision was made for me, things turned out for the better.

It's a hell of a thing to realize your instincts are all wrong, that your heart and your head don't know what you want and couldn't get you there anyway. But fate is there to set things right, at least better than if you were completely in control.

I can't tell my kids this one. I want them to think that their decisions matter, that they have to make a conscious effort to get what they want in life. I want them to be able to make informed decisions, to weigh pros and cons, to be rational and logical, and also to follow their hearts. I don't just want them to be happy, I want them to know they can create their own happiness and take responsibility for it.

Because they're going to have to, because Dad's too busy to do it for them. And he keeps screwing it up anyway.

LESSON 45

NOTHING MATTERS VERY MUCH
AND FEW THINGS MATTER AT ALL

46

RAIN

The best part of a hot summer day in the suburbs wasn't the sun on your face, a cool breeze at your back, or an entire school-less day sprawled out in front of you. No, the best part was hearing that song in the distance...

D'ye ken John Peel with his coat so gay?
D'ye ken John Peel at the break o' day?
D'ye ken John Peel when he's far, far away
With his hounds and his horn in the morning?

That was the song our local ice cream truck played. That was the song we were always listening out for, like Pavlovian dogs. Quick, drop whatever you're doing and run home! Beg your parents for a quarter, *please please please*, all the other kids are getting one, *please please yes!* Run back to the top of the street, hope you're not too late, and join all the other kids hooting and yelping and jumping about like it's the second coming.

That song, that joyous, gleeful song getting louder and louder, the familiar boxy white truck rounding the corner, slowly so as not to run over any out-of-their-mind kids, then coming to a stop as a small mob jockeyed for position and haphazardly formed a line.

What are you having? I had that last time. I want something else! Creamsicle? Fudgsicle? Root beer popsicle!

Really, we didn't need to run to the end of the street. The ice cream man must have known our street was good for 4 to 12 kids every time. Did you ever know one of those guys who wouldn't park for 15 minutes, blaring that music, if he even thought there was a possibility of a sale?

> *For the sound of his horn brought me from my bed,*
> *And the cry of his hounds which he oftime led,*
> *Peel's "View, Halloo!" could awaken the dead,*
> *Or the fox from his lair in the morning.*

One day, it was just me and my sister. I don't remember where everybody else was, but by some fluke, we were the only kids on the street that afternoon when that song, that sweet song...

We got our quarters and rushed to the top of the street. We stood there in anticipation, running down the menu in our heads, weighing our options and gripping our coins, holding them up high as the truck rounded the corner, a tiny silver beacon glinting the way to summer's truest delight!

Hold my hand, sis! I'm your big brother, I take care of you when we're out of Mom's sight. The end of the street is the start of the end of the world and it can be a little tough to handle. You're half my age, too young to be out here on your own. I'm too young to be out here on my own, but I'm old enough to understand why, today, the ice cream truck doesn't stop.

> *D'ye ken John Peel with his coat so gay?*
> *D'ye ken John Peel at the break o' day?*
> *D'ye ken John Peel when he's far, far away*
> *With his hounds and his horn...*

We watch him slowly drive past and away, down, down the street, the back of the truck getting smaller and smaller 'til it rounds the other corner.

Sorry, sis, I couldn't protect you this time. Maybe you're too young to remember. I could pick up the phone and ask you, but what would be the point? Slowly — everything is slow now, this day is going to linger — we trudge back to our house where Mom is talking to a neighbour.

What happened, where's your ice cream? He didn't stop. Maybe he didn't see you? There's nothing else there, Mom. Our neighbour suggests that maybe he didn't know why we were there, we should have held our quarters up high over our heads for the driver to see, and she and Mom demonstrate their technique. We did, we say, just like we do every time. She's a sweet older woman. I don't have the heart nor the stomach to tell her. I can't figure out if my mom feels the same way, if she knows, or if she's been so lulled by the suburbs that she's forgotten.

It wasn't that long ago that you were refused an apartment in town because they didn't rent to "your kind". It wasn't so long ago that your co-worker told you you weren't like those other Chinese, you were one of the good ones. And it wasn't so long ago that I realized there were people out there, past the end of the street, who hated me so much because of what I looked like or who I was or who they thought I was, that they wouldn't even take my money.

30 years ago, in fact. I didn't buy ice cream from an ice cream truck for 30 years.

My son loves ice cream. And you better believe he knows the ice cream truck. It's a different guy, of course, and he plays a different song. We live in a different town, in a different time, in a different world, after all.

I don't think I'll tell my son about that day. I think I'll let him find out for himself. It may never happen to him — wouldn't that be nice? But if it does, I'll let him know that I know how he feels, that it sucks that the world can be like that but it's mostly not, and that there are many, many things in life that are much more important than ice cream.

I really hope he doesn't understand.

LESSON 46
INTO EACH LIFE, SOME RAIN MUST FALL

LESSON
47

SPOIL

We want our kids to be musical, so we bought a piano. When they're old enough, they'll take music lessons just like I did. And, I suppose, they'll hate it too.

I quit my music lessons and stopped playing any musical instruments in high school. Too much studying, it was the perfect excuse. And I didn't miss it, not at all.

But now that we have a piano, I've started playing again. For fun. I got a bunch of our old sheet music that my mom kept and I got some new stuff, songs that I actually know and like and enjoy playing.

I never got it before, that making music could be a joy in and of itself. Instead, my mom used her old fallbacks:

- "I shipped this piano all the way across the country and I'm spending all this money on lessons, so if you don't practice, that's all wasted."
- "Such a beautiful piano. It's an antique, you know. You should feel privileged to play it."
- "You're lucky. I was taught by the nuns. If I didn't arch my hands properly, they'd smack them with a ruler."

I didn't practice because I hated it and I didn't care about the money and nobody smacked my fingers. Then, all these years later, I'm playing again and enjoying it even though I sound terrible and I wish I'd stuck with it.

I'm going to try to make my kids see that knowing how to play an instrument can be fun, that it can be useful in life, that it can give you a greater appreciation for music in general. And if they don't want to practice, I'm going to have to force them with whatever tactics I can muster.

But, obviously, I'm not going to get a ruler. Because in all that time we had the piano, that beautiful antique piano that my mom paid to ship across the country, after all the music lessons, after all the practising and guilt and pain, I never once saw my mom play a single note.

LESSON 47

Spare the rod and spoil the child

LESSON

48

ART

O f all the holidays, Father's Day had to be the worst. A specific, yearly reminder that, *Fuck You*, you don't get to have one. Like I wasn't constantly reminded of that every time I saw some kid with his dad, there had to be a holiday celebrating it?

My least favourite part was having to make a card in school as part of the planned arts and crafts. My teachers were never really prepared for the possibility that someone might be missing a parent, so they'd always suggest I dedicate it to an uncle instead. I had several to choose from, but none were a part of my life in the way that a dad should be, so the sentiment always rang hollow.

I'm pretty sure that I never actually gave them any of the cards, or if I did, they were just as awkward and embarrassed about it as I was. I probably threw them out before I even got home. They just didn't mean anything to me.

One of my uncles actually did teach me how to fish. I learned how to shave from a magazine. I watched a mechanic change a tire, I took woodworking in school, and my mom drove me to soccer games. I had training wheels on my bike, we paid for driving lessons, and I played catch against the side of the house.

Then suddenly, Father's Day became the Best. Holiday. Ever. Because one of those shitty little cards the kids are forced to make in school, whether they have a dad or not, is addressed to me. A crayon-scrawled piece of construction paper with too much white glue and glitter proclaims me to be The Best Daddy In The World and I believe it. I *am* The Best Daddy In The World, I'm always going to be The Best Daddy In The World, because I'm always going to be there for you.

I'm sure my dad thought so, too. He never got any cards — he died when I was too young to make any.

Nowadays, kids are missing parents all the time. Divorced, never married, lost to cancer, single moms, or maybe they have two of one and none of the other. Teachers are much better equipped to deal with all the different permutations of families than when I was a kid. Our whole society is.

So if anything ever happens to me and I'm not there anymore, you'll be in better hands than I was. You might still have to make a card, though.

If you do, please make it out to me, no matter what they tell you to do. And please, please, don't throw the cards away.

LESSON 48

ALL ART IS QUITE USELESS

LESSON
49

DIAMONDS

My co-worker Mary's son is, according to her, very smart. Some would even say, 'gifted'. She certainly does, every chance she gets.

Like this job isn't bad enough without her prattling on and on about him. Dead-end, low-rung, shit-paying jobs can be tolerable if you like your co-workers. She's nice enough… she just has this one annoying habit.

"Oh, I have to go pick Adam up from *gifted*. He was telling me the other day how he thinks he can make the space shuttle more efficient. That's the kind of thing they study in *gifted*! He still doesn't know what he wants to do when he grows up. He has so many options, though. That's the advantage of being *gifted*!"

Yeah, I get it. You're proud of your son. He's smart — that's great. Intelligence isn't valued enough in our society. If he's as smart as you say he is, we're going to need him. But beyond that, I don't care.

My kids have their positive traits, but I don't go around bragging about them all the time. And if they were 'gifted', I wouldn't build them up like that. Too much pressure, too high expectations, and a kid can get stressed, be anxious, flame out. I want my kids to succeed, but not at the expense of their happiness and well-being.

She's doing it again. This has to stop.

"Mary," I tell her, "*I* was gifted."

She stops.

I'm sure her son will do fine. I hope my kids will, too.

The job still sucks, though.

LESSON 49

NO PRESSURE, NO DIAMONDS

LESSON

50

ENDS

My brother-in-law is raising his kids the way he was raised because he turned out just fine, according to him.

Now, there's a trap I never want to fall into. I think I'm a pretty decent dad, but there's always room for improvement. I know I have problems — nothing major, my kids seem happy and well-adjusted so far — but I haven't thought I was perfect in a long time.

My childhood wasn't bad. In fact, most of it was probably pretty happy. But there are definitely things I would change if I could. I suppose that's how I'm raising my kids — using my own upbringing as a template, but with added tweaks and improvements. With love, care, and kindness, but with a little more thoughtfulness. And empathy. And second-guessing.

My brother-in-law and I were raised differently, but we both turned out fine. Well, he thinks I'm a piece of shit and I think he has anger issues, but our kids are going to be fantastic, if our own opinions of our own parenting is any kind of a predictor.

I'm sure our kids will have something to say about their childhoods when they're older, but for now, I'm content to sit back and wait to be proven right. My brother-in-law isn't. He tells me what I'm doing wrong every time I see him. I pretend to agree with him, then do the opposite of what he told me to do, right in front of him, just to piss him off.

But I guess that's what people who were raised right and turned out just fine do to each other.

LESSON 50
ALL'S WELL THAT ENDS WELL

LESSON
51

END

I've never liked saying 'Goodbye'. Not the act, the actual word. There's a finality to it, a feeling that the person I'm saying it to is leaving my life forever. And while there have been people I've said 'Goodbye' to because they were leaving forever, to most people in most situations I've always said 'See you'.

That's much more preferable, for obvious reasons. There's a sense of continuation, that I'll see you again tomorrow or next week or at least someday. I'm not ready to let you go, you're to stay in my life for at least a while longer, we'll cross paths again.

And then my mom tells me that 'See you' were the last words my father ever said to her before he went off to work that day and never came back.

Even knowing this, I still can't shake the habit. I still say 'See you' to everybody, including my mom. And every time I say it to her, there's a part of my mind that stumbles over itself a little.

Is it painful for her to hear it? Should I say something else? Does she feel the same sense of continuation that I do, that the person saying it will see her again? Could it be the reason why, after all these years, she has never remarried?

I know that one day I'll say 'See you' to her and that'll be the last time I ever see her. Perhaps, as we all get older, I'll start saying 'Goodbye', but not yet. I'm not ready to let go just yet. Or maybe I'll never stop saying 'See you' and life will go on and on, forever and ever, and I won't even notice.

LESSON 51

ALL GOOD THINGS MUST COME TO AN END

LESSON

52

KNOW

There have been many different times in my life when I pretended not to know something. Different ages, different reasons, different results.

As a small child, I pretended not to know things because I realized the grown-ups would be more open and they would disclose their secrets if they thought you didn't understand them.

In grade school, I pretended not to know things because I realized I was a lot smarter than the other kids — and some of the adults, too.

In high school, I pretended not to know things, mainly to avoid embarrassment or getting beat up.

As a young adult, I pretended not to know things because I needed to cover up mistakes or shift blame.

And now, as a more mature adult, I pretend not to know things because I'm usually tired and I'd like to dodge as much responsibility as I can.

My son is pretty smart, but he doesn't like to show it. He knows how to read, but he won't because he likes it when we read to him, which is actually pretty sweet when you think about it.

I guess he's taking after his dad and he's got a lifetime of

pretending not to know things ahead of him. I can't fault him
— I'd rather he was pretending not to know than to actually not
know things.

So I'm pretending not to know that he's pretending not to
know. What I don't know is if he knows I'm pretending not to
know that he knows. And if I find out, should I let him know or
should I keep on pretending?

Kid's only five and I think he's outsmarted me already.
Whatever I do, I can't let him know that...

LESSON 52

IT TAKES ONE TO KNOW ONE

LESSON

53

DARES

On my 15th birthday, the world did not end.

My mom took me and a few friends out for pizza, then we watched *Return of the Jedi* at the local theatre. For a few hours, I forgot I was a depressed, pimply, wildly-unpopular high school nerd. Instead, I was the swashbuckling hero, battling my way across the galaxy against insurmountable odds, defeating the forces of evil amid lots of cool-looking explosions and laser fire.

Meanwhile, on the other side of the globe, a Soviet officer named Stanislav Petrov actually saved the entire fucking world.

In September 1983, American–Soviet relations were strained to say the least. Caught up in the Mutually Assured Destruction mindset, each country kept building up their nuclear arsenals with more missiles, better missiles, capable of hitting more targets farther away more quickly. U.S. president Ronald Reagan was playing a dangerous game, flying bombers right up to Soviet airspace, then turning back at the last minute. The Soviets actually shot down a South Korean passenger jet that accidentally crossed over, killing all on board, including many Americans and a U.S. congressman. Both sides were on edge, constantly monitoring their early-warning systems for that first shot, the first of many missiles, knowing that they only had a few minutes to retaliate with a massive strike of their own, which would surely kill hundreds of millions of people on both sides, injure and maim many more, and plunge the world into a nuclear winter for decades, if not centuries.

I, on the other hand, had just started grade 10 and was unaware of such machinations. I was more concerned with getting good grades, keeping my head down, and not getting beat up before, between, or after classes. The threat of nuclear annihilation was always there and I was scared of it — we all were — it just wasn't the fear that demanded the most of my attention at the time.

Mr. Petrov was the duty officer at the Oko nuclear early-warning system's command centre on September 26, 1983 when it suddenly showed five missiles launched from the U.S.

Protocol dictated that he should notify his commanders, who would most likely follow their orders and launch a massive retaliatory strike. However, Petrov kept his cool and, after a few tense minutes, decided against contacting them. He knew the launch detection system was new and he didn't trust it, he reasoned that five was an oddly small number of missiles to start an attack with, and I like to think he was also a decent human being who didn't want to overreact and snuff out a good chunk of life on Earth. Obviously, he was right on all counts. The system had, in fact, malfunctioned.

On-screen, fireworks and fly-bys celebrated the defeat of the Empire and the destruction of the second Death Star. Mr. Petrov was at first praised by his superiors, but then quietly demoted, receiving no reward nor recognition for his actions — or inactions — for over twenty years. I went to school the next day, successfully evading detection of a different sort.

The threat of nuclear weapons is still with us, but it just doesn't feel as scary as it did in the '80s. It's not that they're any less deadly — quite the opposite — but there are so many other threats, newer threats, over which to spread our fears, it's kind of taken a backseat. And, personally, I'm no longer afraid of dying in a flash of light anymore. I'm more afraid that something bad could happen to my kids. Car accidents, random stabbings, childhood leukemia — this is what keeps me awake at night now.

My kids are at the age when they're afraid of monsters. As they get older, their fears will progress and mature, as mine did, and we'll face them together. Perhaps they'll be afraid of nuclear annihilation, perhaps it'll remain a vague, omnipresent threat, too immense to grasp fully or even contemplate.

But I'll tell them about Stanislav Petrov and how he saved the world by doing nothing, because it's soothing to feel there are good men and women out there, looking out for us and making the hard decisions. And I'll tell them that I did nothing too, so maybe I also saved the world, who's to say? And they can be heroes and do nothing as well, and that'll keep them safe and Daddy won't have to be quite so afraid all the time.

So... who's up for a movie?

LESSON 53
HE WHO DARES, WINS

LESSON
54
BEGINNING

For the first few months of fatherhood, I just didn't get it. I was a terrible father, I admit it. I didn't understand that here was this little life that was dependent on me for so much.

Thankfully, my wife had prepared and was up to it. She had done the research and cared for our son and fed and changed him while I was determined to not let this little interloper interfere with my normal routine.

I think part of it was that I had never really wanted kids. I wasn't wholly against it, I just never thought it was something I needed to do.

Who was this little asshole who couldn't speak, yet demanded so much? I resented him and what he represented: the end of my youth, of growing up and maturing, an unwelcome responsibility, my loss of freedom.

And so I kept myself away. He'd cry and I'd ignore it, knowing my wife would tend to him. He'd need a diaper change and I'd leave it for her. I'd happily go to work in the morning, returning as late as I could each night.

But wouldn't you know, the cute little guy grew on me. As he got older and more interesting, I started paying more attention. And as I did, I started spending more time with him. And as I did that, I started becoming a better father.

Today, I'm totally devoted to him. Looking at us, you'd never guess how shaky our relationship was at the beginning. And it was all my fault.

So, pretty much the opposite of my marriage.

LESSON 54
BEGINNING IS EASY; CONTINUING, HARD

LESSON
55

MEDIOCRE

I praise my kids too much. I know I do. But I want them to have good self-esteem and a strong sense of self-worth.

I don't remember my mom ever praising me. I remember constant criticism. Nothing was ever acceptable, I could always do better if I'd only try harder. And it was just me, my little sister wasn't subjected to that. I always thought that was so unfair.

They say kids today have too much confidence, an inflated sense of themselves, yet they have no actual accomplishments. When they get out in the world, reality comes crashing down and they get depressed, frustrated, withdrawn.

I'm pretty smart, but I never had any confidence, so I never tried. I didn't think I could succeed because I wasn't good enough. I never took any chances because I didn't want to fail again.

I have to strike a balance with my kids. Give them enough confidence to want to try, enough subtle criticism to make them want to try harder.

If I can do that, then I suppose that will be my success. If I fail, then I'll have failed again. I have to really try this time because I *have* to. Otherwise, they could end up just like me.

I know my mom just wanted me to do my best and keep trying

harder and succeed. But what if she didn't like what she saw and didn't want me to be me? That kind of backfired, didn't it?

Good job there, Mom. I know you were well-intentioned, but you should have been smarter than that. Couldn't you see it wasn't working, that I was so unhappy? Well, I guess you did, because you adjusted your strategy. You certainly succeeded with my younger sister.

There, just like that. This parenting shit is easy.

LESSON 55

ONLY THE MEDIOCRE ARE ALWAYS AT THEIR BEST

LESSON
56

MEMORIES

y earliest memory is sitting on the stairs.
My second-earliest memory is sitting in a box.
My third-earliest memory is sitting on a toilet.
My fourth-earliest memory is sitting up in bed.
My fifth-earliest memory is sitting on a bench.

In my earliest memory, I'm sitting on the stairs, waiting for my dad to come home.

In my second-earliest memory, I'm sitting in a box at the warehouse my dad owned.

In my third-earliest memory, I'm at my uncle and aunt's house.

In my fourth-earliest memory, I'm still at my uncle and aunt's house.

In my fifth-earliest memory, I'm in a courtroom.

In my earliest memory, my dad comes home, scoops me up off the stairs into his arms, and hugs me. It's so clear to me still, after all these years — the anticipation, the joy of seeing him, the comfort, the yellow shag carpet on the stairs, his thin red plasticky jacket with the white liner. I'm happy.

In my second-earliest memory, I'm being slid around in a cardboard box on the conveyor belt at my dad's warehouse. He's the one doing the sliding. My mom and grandmother are there, too. I'm having fun, but I get concerned when my grandmother drops some of the candy my dad has given her. But that part is fleeting, I'm exuberant from the sensation of gliding back and forth, back and forth. Everyone I love is there.

In my third-earliest memory, I'm on the toilet because I've just shit my pants.

In my fourth-earliest memory, I've just had a nightmare. I whimper and call out for my mother. My uncle and aunt are at the door, looking in. I see them, remember where I am, and lie back down again. I don't want them.

In my fifth-earliest memory, I don't understand what's going on but I'm terrified.

In my fourth-earliest memory, in my nightmare, my mother is leaving me. She's being driven away in a car with an unseen driver. She won't look at me or tell me where she's going or even when or if she'll be back.

In my third-earliest memory, I'm confused, scared, and almost overwhelmingly sad. The door to the bathroom is open and my grandmother looks in. She's sad, too. I turn away from her because it's just too much.

In my fifth-earliest memory, there's a man on the stand in the courtroom, looking around with disdain and indifference. I'm eating dry cereal out of a lunchbox.

My mom would tell me how my dad would take me to the warehouse and slide me around on the conveyor belt in a box, just like in my second-earliest memory. The thing is, he never once took my grandmother.

In my third-earliest memory, my uncle has just yelled at me for shitting my pants. He thought that was disgusting and unacceptable. I was two and a half years old.

Later that week, in my fourth-earliest memory, my nightmare

of my mother leaving probably came about because when my father was murdered, she sent me to my uncle and aunt's for two weeks and I didn't understand why. There, I shit my pants and got yelled at.

My grandmother remembers looking in on me in the bathroom. The sight of me sitting there, so small and so sad, she said it broke her heart.

My dad never owned a thin red plasticky jacket with a white liner. There was a boy I used to play with when I was a bit older who did.

If my two earliest memories are false, dreams that I had, lies that I told myself, the earliest memories I wished I had but don't, then what does that make me?

My son is about the age I was when my earliest memory should have happened. I want his first memory to be a happy one. I can't control what he'll remember, nobody can, but I'm going to do my best to provide him with many happy moments to choose from.

My sixth-earliest memory is talking to a hole. I'm walking in the snow with my mom. There's a small hole beside the pathway. I'm a bit of a goof, so I start talking to it.

"Hello, Mr. Hole. How are you today?"

She remembers it. There's a photo of me doing it. It's a silly moment that made my mom laugh.

I could start there.

LESSON 56

YOU ARE THE SUM OF YOUR MEMORIES

LESSON
57

FIRST

I was never good at sports: I wasn't very well-coordinated, I was a little chubby, I never scored the winning goal, or all that many goals for that matter. I always seemed to be on the losing team — I probably didn't help much there. But I do have one moment of sports-related glory.

It was the third-last high school Phys. Ed. class I'd ever have to take and I couldn't have been more relieved. The years of near-daily humiliation were close to coming to an end. This year had been particularly difficult because of our teacher, Mr. V.

Nobody liked Mr. V., a barrel-chested man with stick legs and a creepy moustache who took a dim view of those of us who were not athletically-gifted. Sometimes he'd join in whatever game we were playing, perhaps out of boredom, perhaps to show off.

On the third-last day, we were playing softball. I hated this activity because everybody could see you suck individually as well as on a team. Mr. V. was pitching for both sides that day. A welcome consideration — the other team had a kid who played in a league and could strike out pretty much any of us with some crazy fast underhand pitch.

I actually managed to get on base that day with a single. A

few other hitters got me all the way over to third. A weak single stranded me there and loaded the bases. The next hit, I had no choice, I had to run for home. It wouldn't be a winning run, but it would be an actual run, more than I usually got.

I don't remember who was at bat. I was leaning forward as far as I could, focussed on home plate and getting there safely. *Crack!* and I was off, running as fast as my chubby body would go, my glasses bouncing around my face, my leaden feet clumping too slowly for such a long distance.

Another weak single, right to Mr. V.! He easily scooped up the ball. He looked over at me running — there was plenty of time to throw to the catcher and get me out. But, for some reason, perhaps to intensify my humiliation, perhaps just to show off, he decided to run it in.

It was going to be close, but I think he was slightly closer to home than I was. I didn't want to be out at home, to make it all that way and then fail, but I couldn't go back either. I was resigning myself mid-run to not scoring — again — when I heard over the din someone yelling, "Slide! Slide!"

I had never slid into home before. I might have seen it done once or twice on TV, but I wasn't even entirely sure how to actually do it properly. Yet, somehow, I managed to execute a perfect slide. I threw myself down, ending up with my feet against the plate and my legs weren't even scratched, despite wearing shorts. I'm not sure if I beat Mr. V. there or not, but it didn't matter.

When I slid in, he either tripped over me or my feet kicked his out from under him. He did a complete forward somersault through the air, landing heavily on his rear end in the dirt and a large cloud of dust, the dropped ball bouncing away from him. And all the boys — on both teams — threw their hands in the air and cheered.

I didn't care that I was safe at home. I was mortified. My teammates all crowded around, laughing and congratulating me and clapping me on the back. I, on the other hand, was trying to hide behind them, away from Mr. V.'s glowering stare.

I didn't have another at-bat that game and I spent the last two Phys. Ed. classes of my life being as invisible as possible. My main concern, more than his in-class retribution, was that he was going to fail me. I was trying to get into university and I couldn't afford a bad grade dragging my GPA down — in P.E., no less! But when report cards came out, I'd gotten a B, as good a grade as I could have hoped for. I don't know if it was an act of mercy, forgiveness, or if I'd somehow finally earned his begrudging respect, but I wasn't about to go finding out. I went on to university, where I failed some more, but at least not on the sports field.

So that's my one sports story. Looking back, I'm kind of glad I wasn't good at sports. I'd hate to have a whole bunch of these stories that I'd tell and retell over and over, reliving the moments again and again, sadly basking in faded glory and long-forgotten adulation.

If my kids go out for sports, if they turn out to be athletically gifted, I'll go to their games and cheer them on and support them in general. And I'll feign interest in their sports stories and laugh along at the right parts. And maybe I'll tell my story sometimes. It's a decent story, but it's my only one and that can only take you so far.

But, chances are, they'll be more like me. They won't like sports and will rather bury their noses in books. That's okay, lots of good stories in those. Maybe not their own, actual stories, but they're more likely to get into university that way.

And, of course, they'd be more impressed by my one sports story if they had none of their own.

LESSON 57
SECOND PLACE IS JUST THE FIRST LOSER

LESSON
58

MIND

Something I hated when I was a kid was when adults would talk about me in front of me as if I wasn't there or as if I couldn't hear or understand them.

It happened with troubling regularity, but I figured out pretty quickly that if I pretended to ignore them, I could learn things. Things that maybe I wasn't supposed to be privy to. What people thought of me. Adult stuff.

So I'd eavesdrop, but it wasn't really spying because I was right there, making no effort to hide, and they were making no effort to avoid me or to mask their conversations.

And over the years I learned some things, but mostly I learned two things: adults are idiots and they seemed to think I was an idiot, too.

Sometimes I forget my kids understand me because there were a number of years when they didn't. And I catch myself talking about them in front of them and I catch them pretending to ignore me. But I don't call them on it — that would be hypocritical.

Instead, I start talking about how smart and wonderful they are and how well they're doing, then I try to slip in some interesting factoid about the world. Might as well get something educational in while I have their attention.

Heaven knows they don't listen to anything else I say.

LESSON 58
MIND YOUR OWN BUSINESS

LESSON

59·60

ALL · MAN

It didn't take much to make Davey cry. Any perceived slight or hint of criticism, any minor failure or frustration, any obstacle or inconvenience, and the tears would start to flow. He'd try to hold them in at first, but he never succeeded, despite all the practice.

He was a nice kid, I liked him — we all did — but secretly, he disgusted me. All his fussing over nothing, I thought he was pathetic and weak. He'd get an answer wrong in class or something and his eyes would well up and everybody would start reassuring him that it was okay — he'd almost got it right, he'd get it next time, it wasn't a big deal — he'd cry for a bit and then we'd move on. Until the next time, sometimes several times a day, pretty much every day.

Sometime after I left that school, I heard through the grapevine that his mother had cancer. Then I heard that she had died. And I hated myself for thinking it, but I thought, well, now he finally has something worth crying over.

My son cries more than I'd like, but then, he's five. I want him to be in touch with his sensitive side, but not *too* much.

119

Somewhere between Davey and Dad, because either end of that spectrum is a pretty terrible place to be.

LESSON 59
IT'S ALL RIGHT TO CRY

LESSON 60
BE A MAN

LESSON
61
MISTAKES

I love videogames. I've been playing them a long time, since I was a kid. My kids will probably play them too. I'm totally fine with that.

I love how I can be somebody else, completely different from who I am in real life. I can go anywhere, do anything, take risks that I would never actually take.

But I think my favourite feature of videogames is the 'save game'. In most games, if I save my progress, I can reload from that point and try again. So if I die in the game or screw up really bad or just want to do part of it over, I can go back and do it again as many times as I want, until I get it right.

I couldn't tell you how many times I've wished there was something like that in real life. Unlimited do-overs, the ability to erase all my mistakes — I could live the perfect life with no regrets, take all the risks, and reap only the rewards.

Just the other night, I was playing videogames downstairs into the wee hours while my family slept. I started getting tired, so I shut everything down, started on my way up to bed, and promptly ripped my pants.

Noooo! I screamed, not too loud so the family wouldn't wake, *not my favourite pants!*

I don't have very many pairs left that fit me — I've gained a bit of weight lately *(shut up)* — now I'm going to have to go out and buy a new pair. That's money I didn't need to spend.

I was just playing a videogame. Why can't I reload? Why can't I go back in time, just a bit, and redo the last minute so I don't rip my pants? Why can't I go back twenty or thirty years and relive my life, but this time make all the right decisions? Because time, and life, don't work that way, that's why.

And then I woke up. To my videogame still playing at the point where I'd been when I drifted off. But, more importantly, to unripped pants.

"Yesss!" I shouted, a bit too loud, waking my family up.

LESSON 61

THE MAN WHO MAKES NO MISTAKES DOES NOT USUALLY MAKE ANYTHING

LESSON

62

VIOLENCE

"What was my dad like?"
    "He had such a bad temper."

My dad died when I was two and a half years old, so all I knew of him was secondhand. I hungrily absorbed any information I could get about him, good or bad. Mostly good, except for one negative trait that was emphasized repeatedly by my mother.

I know why she said it. She saw so much of him in me, she didn't want me to turn out like that, at least not like the worst part of his personality. Except it backfired.

A young boy learns how to behave from his father. In the absence of a father, he might emulate his memory or his reputation.

So I had a bad temper, such a bad temper. And that worried my mother, who must have been so desperate to control me that she told me I was going to be a wife-beater when I grew up.

Now, this was different. I never saw any wife-beating at home, only on TV, where the wife-beater was just about the worst villain you could imagine. She scared me, and I scared myself, as to what I could become, what I could already be.

So I stayed away from women and I didn't date. I avoided relationships with them to protect them from me, from what I was destined to become, because even my mom could see it.

My dad never hit my mom. She idolized him. They were only married for about five years, not long enough for animosities to grow, for resentments to develop. She always spoke about him and his accomplishments in the most glowing of terms, except...

"He had such a bad temper."

I hear from other people about their dads, I read other accounts, and I watch TV shows and movies about horrible, abusive husbands who beat their wives and horrible, abusive dads who beat their kids, then I wonder briefly if maybe, just maybe, I'm better off for not ever having known him.

Then I dismiss that entirely. I've had enough fatherless moments in my life to know I would have done anything, put up with anything, endured anything to have had the chance to grow up with him.

A young boy learns how to behave from his father. In the absence of a father, he might emulate his memory or his reputation.

So I had a bad temper and I was alone. And when I finally allowed myself to start dating women, I never even thought of raising a hand against any of them.

Because even though my dad had a bad temper, such a bad temper, he never hit my mom.

Right?

I never saw it. It was never discussed. I never talked about it with her, I could *never* talk about it with her. I couldn't besmirch his memory, his reputation, or allow her to do so.

"He had such a bad temper."

My wife and I fight. My kids and I fight. But they're all safe in the knowledge that I'll never, ever hit them. That's just not who or what I am, not who or what I was raised to be.

You'll never convince me that I'm better off for my not having known my dad. But maybe, just maybe, my wife and kids are.

LESSON 62

VIOLENCE BEGETS VIOLENCE

LESSON

63

LUCK

When I was a kid, for some insane reason, my grandmother told me that Chinese people believed if you blew on your food to cool it down, you were blowing away all your good luck.

I have a kid now who's not too fussy an eater, but he screams bloody murder if his dinner is anything above room temperature. Blowing on his food is a necessity if we want to get him to bed on time.

I was *not* a fussy eater. If anything, I was quite enthusiastic, so I spent a good part of my childhood with a burnt tongue. I used to wonder if China was a country full of people with burnt tongues.

In her later years, I tried asking my grandmother why she told me this, but her mind was slipping away and she couldn't remember. So I guess I'll never know why.

But I do know that it's true. I'm the luckiest guy around! I have a fantastic kid who eats all his dinner right up every night.

As long as I blow on it.

LESSON 63

YOU MAKE YOUR OWN LUCK

LESSON

64

COUNT

S itting in the back of a car, as an adult, is kind of novel
for me. My wife doesn't drive, so I'm always up front, her
beside me, kids in back. When I look back at them, they
seem content but I wonder if they're itching to get up front.

That's where the adults sit, after all. Being up front means
you're grown up, you're in charge, in control. In back means
you're a helpless passenger, you have no say in where you're
going, you can barely even see where you're going. Who wouldn't
want to give that up?

Sometimes I sit in the back seat, perhaps when I'm cleaning
the car and it's not moving, and I get a giddy little rush. And I'll
sit and look out the window and remember what it was like to
not have to watch where I'm going, to not have to be careful of
traffic and pedestrians and freeway exits, to have someone else
making all the decisions and handling the responsibilities and
keeping me safe. Who'd want to give that up?

We've got a good decade before any of the kids are getting
behind the wheel. Then another decade or two before my eyes
start to fail and my body gives out. Then, maybe they can drive
me around for a change. Maybe I'll even sit in the back seat. And
I'll just sit and look out the window and finally take my eyes off

the road.

Maybe I won't get a little rush, it'll be more like a tinge of resignation. But I'll be ready to give up control. If we've done our job and raised them right and they're good drivers and responsible adults, I'll be okay with them in charge.

Whenever I drive my mom someplace, she complains constantly: I'm driving too fast, too recklessly, watch where I'm going, be more careful. She still drives on her own, but her eyes are going, her body is giving out. Perhaps she doesn't want to give up control just yet. Or perhaps she still doesn't trust me completely.

Poor thing, never had much faith in herself.

LESSON 64

DON'T COUNT YOUR CHICKENS BEFORE THEY HATCH

65

HARD

I still have all my old high school yearbooks. I don't look at them much. No real reason to.

It was not an enjoyable experience for me: I was a nerd, I was picked on, I had a few other friends who were also nerds and kind of assholes. I did okay academically but sucked at sports and socially. I remember being scared, worried, and depressed a lot.

I was weird-looking. That haircut, those glasses, that sad attempt at a moustache. Not much interest in clothes and it showed. I thought my skin would clear up, I'd grow into my body, maybe my face would change as I got older, and I'd become handsome. I wasn't yet resigned to looking this bad for the rest of my life.

Worst of all is, looking at my old pictures, I still had hope. I thought my best years were still to come. I had grand plans, expectations for myself, and the initiative and drive to make them happen. Seeing the optimism in that young kid's eyes hurts a little too much. I don't need the extra introspection, more late-night self-loathing, the endless rounds of the where-did-I-go-wrong game.

My son is about to embark on his school career. I hope he does better than I did. I hope he has more fun. I hope he makes better friends, I hope he lives up to his potential, I hope he'll have better memories of the experience than I do.

And when the time comes, we'll buy him his high school yearbook so, good or bad, he can preserve those memories and look back at them as often as he wishes. But not too often. We want him to keep looking forward, keep looking forward, with those bright, beautiful, hope-filled eyes of his.

If he ever does get resigned, if he ever does quit trying, if he ever forgets his optimism and his initiative and his drive, I'll get his old yearbook and show him his old pictures. We'll talk about that young boy and who he used to be, who he became, and who he could still become.

Then I'll close the book up and smack him with it until he finds his way again.

LESSON 65

IT'S HARD TO BEAT A PERSON WHO NEVER GIVES UP

LESSON
66
GOOD

For every stage my son hit, I thought, "This is it, this is the best. This is the best it's going to be."

The first two or three months were horrible. He was so weak and helpless and he just ate, pooped, and cried. But then he got some neck control and it wasn't so scary to simply hold him anymore, which was such a relief. I could put him down somewhere and leave him for a bit — he couldn't go anywhere, so I always knew where he was.

Then he started sitting up and that was fun. He'd kick his legs, roll around, flail his arms, and eventually tumble the right way and surprise himself. Very entertaining and he still stayed where I left him, more or less. And I thought, "This is so much better now."

Then he started crawling and that was cool — the pure joy on his face when he realized he wasn't stuck in one place anymore. I could still stop him from going too far with some strategically placed pillows and he became so much better at keeping himself occupied because he could get to all his toys.

Then he got to the stage I was dreading and started standing, but it turned out to be the best yet. It was amazing to watch him teeter to his feet, grabbing the couch for support, and lurching around the living room. I'd reach out for his outstretched hand, he'd collapse into my arms with a big smile of accomplishment, and I'd just melt.

When he started walking on his own, that was great because I didn't have to carry him quite so much anymore. But that was nothing compared to talking. Just a few words at first, then sentences, then actually making his intentions known instead of just crying and us guessing. But that paled next to completing toilet training, for obvious reasons.

Now he walks and talks and feeds himself and goes to the bathroom without us. He's his own little man and his own little personality and it's awesome, truly the best stage yet. I don't really think about what's coming next, but I'm having trouble imagining how it could possibly get better than this. I'm sure it will, though.

But now we have a little girl. A crying, pooping, immobile, wordless little girl. And it feels like our whole family has taken a huge step backwards. I can't help but look at her and think, "This is the worst stage. This is the worst it's ever going to be." But I know what's coming, and what's after that, and after that, so I can't help but smile like an idiot as she burbles and coos and then vomits all down my shirt.

My son sees this and says "I'll help you, Daddy" as he runs off to get the paper towels, and I'm so giddy with anticipation I can hardly breathe.

LESSON 66

THESE ARE THE GOOD OLD DAYS

67

WORK

M y wife and I have toyed with the idea of opening an
ice cream shop. It would have to be like one of those
old-fashioned ones from the '70s, soft-serve only, with
chocolate-dipped cones and banana splits and lots of chopped
nuts and sprinkles. There was one we loved near our old house,
but nothing like it in our new city. We think it could do very well.

But then, I suppose our kids would become those Chinese
kids who are always hanging out at their parents' shop. Not that
there's anything wrong with that — we have a quietly proud
tradition of it. You see it all the time in small corner stores or
restaurants, the owner's children squatting on a milk crate near
the back room, doing their homework there after school because
where else are they going to go? Both parents are at the store,
working.

There was a certain restaurant in Vancouver, a steakhouse,
that we passed whenever we drove into town. We used to joke
that it must be mafia-owned because we never saw anybody go
in or come out and there were never any cars in the parking lot.
It was there for years, as long as I could remember. One day,
when I knew I was moving away, I went in for dinner. I had to
know before I left.

It was run by an old Chinese couple, the original owners, and it probably still had the original décor. The husband cooked and the wife waited the tables. She glommed on to me and told me the entire history of the place, how they served mostly dockworkers and the poorer denizens of the neighbourhood, people who perhaps didn't have cars.

They worked long hours, late hours, and served plain but affordable fare. However, she was most proud of her two sons, who grew up in the restaurant, probably sitting at the table at the back nearest the kitchen. One was now a doctor, the other a lawyer. I had a perfectly serviceable $10 steak with some bland vegetables that probably came from a tin. I tipped extra well and left with a full feeling, one of life's mysteries solved.

So if my kids grow up like that, I wouldn't have a problem with it. They'd hang out at the ice cream shop after school and help out as they got older. Who knows, it might even make them really popular with their friends. Then, when the time came, I'd either hand the business down to them or send them off into the world.

We're not too sure about the long, late hours, though. Most of that would fall to me and I'm not sure I'm up to it. And neither of us has any actual experience owning and operating a business or even selling ice cream, just eating it. It's starting to look like a pipe dream, fanciful thinking.

I hate to think that's the reason my kids won't grow up to be doctors or lawyers. It's one thing to push them to succeed, it's another thing entirely to push yourself to push them to succeed. I'm ready to sacrifice for my kids, as long as it's not too inconvenient. And that's really not the attitude to have in the service industry.

LESSON 67

A LITTLE HARD WORK NEVER HURT ANYBODY

68

PRESERVE

There are more photos of my son in his first month than there are of me in my entire life.

When I was growing up, there were no digital cameras, just film. And buying film cost money and developing film cost money — we weren't rich, so you had to get your money's worth with every shot.

There are no candid moments from my childhood. Every photograph is carefully staged and posed, almost always taking place during a special occasion, a family get-together like Christmas or a birthday party.

And all the shots are the same. Line the kids up, shortest to tallest, squeeze everybody in there, everybody smile, and that's it. One photo, maybe two. A roll of twelve would last us years.

Here's a bunch of photos of my son the day he was born. Here he is the next day. Here's one of him eating, here he is sleeping, here he's sitting up, here he's just looking around. By the end of his first month, he knew what the camera was and responded with a smile each time, the little ham.

I look back on my childhood with fondness, but it has to be through memory. All the photos of it are phony and artificial, our bodies and faces stiff and insincere.

Then I look at my parents' photos and realize how good we had it. There are maybe half a dozen pictures of my mom's whole childhood, even fewer of my dad. A baby photo, a portrait with siblings, high school graduation, first car. The milestones were documented, but the little moments had to fall away.

My kids won't have that problem, we're recording everything, video too. And I wonder how it's going to affect their memories of their childhood. How can you remember something when I can just pull up the video and show you exactly what happened?

I worry that I might actually be recording too much. Perhaps there are moments they'll want to forget, something embarrassing or unpleasant. Or perhaps the memory of an event would be better than it actually was. I've seen movies and TV shows that I thought were amazing as a child but turned out to be cheesy and lame upon viewing them as an adult. Memories could be like that, too.

I'm erring on the side of caution. Because even if they never want to look at their old photos, I will, especially if it all goes sour. They could turn out all wrong and hate me, move far away and never speak to me again, but I have enough photos and videos that I could retreat to the past and just stay there. Which is what I'd probably be doing right now in my head, if I didn't have such awesome kids.

I really do. And I have the photos to prove it.

LESSON 68

PRESERVE YOUR MEMORIES, THEY'RE ALL THAT'S LEFT YOU

LESSON

69

OTHERS

Stop teasing your little sister. It's not very nice. She doesn't like it.

Stop making faces at your little sister. You're upsetting her. Your face is going to stick that way. Please don't do that anymore.

Stop calling your little sister names. You're hurting her feelings. She's more sensitive than you are. That's a beautiful thing. You should treasure it.

Stop stealing your little sister's toys. They're hers, you have your own. Respect her property. You should respect all people's property. That's common courtesy. How would you feel if someone did that to you?

Stop poking your little sister. That's very irritating. You're going to make her cry. You don't want to make her cry, do you? Why would you want to do that? Why be cruel when you can be kind? You should make the world a better place by being here, not worse.

Stop sitting on your little sister. You're much bigger than she is. That's not a fair fight. You're being a bully. You shouldn't pick on smaller kids just because you can. You're not proving anything to the world except that you're inconsiderate of other people's feelings. And you're not impressing anybody. Wow, an unfair fight, you're a real hero.

Stop pulling your little sister's hair. Do you know what karma is? That's when the universe gets back at you for all the bad things you've done. You should do good things, so good things will happen to you in return. You could be an example of how to behave. This is beneath you, you're better than this. You should be protecting her. She looks up to you. Don't betray her trust.

Stop hitting your little sister. You're going to hurt her. How would you feel if you seriously injured her? You'd feel terrible. Yes, you would. She's your sister for life. She will always be there. One day, when your mother and I are gone, she'll be the only link you have to the past. Believe it or not, these are some of the best years of your life. You should make the most of them, for both of you.

If you don't stop beating up your little sister right this instant — if I hear even one more peep, or one more whimper, or if there is just one more tear shed, if I have to turn around and you're not both happy smiling angels, if she even *looks* uncomfortable, if you can't keep your hands to yourself, if you keep this up, if she's hurt in any way, if anything ever happens to her, I swear to God — *You're next.*

LESSON 69

DO UNTO OTHERS AS YOU WOULD HAVE THEM DO UNTO YOU

LESSON
70
TREASURE

My wife lost my favourite pen. Well, gave it away. A contractor working at the house needed to write something down, so she went into my desk and gave him one of my pens, not realizing it was my favourite. Then he left it at his next job, who knows where. It's gone now and I can't get it back.

My friend Ali in college gave me that pen. Well, I made him buy it for me after he lost the one I lent him. It was funny at the time to make him do that, to find an exact replacement. He went along with the joke too, going to a half-dozen different stationery stores to find the exact model. Gift-wrapped it with a bow and everything.

Six months later, he died in a car accident. Young boys on the cusp of adulthood suddenly having to deal with death, some of us handled it better than others. At the funeral, I couldn't introduce myself to his family. I sat alone in the corner of the church, not talking to anybody. When I signed the book of condolences, I realized I was using the pen, then cried alone in my car.

I made my wife replace the pen. Well, I asked her to and she did, but I didn't tell her why it was my favourite. She went to exactly one store. It's a fine pen, but it's not the same pen. I don't even know if they still make them. I wasn't going to make her hunt it down, it just didn't feel like it would be funny this time.

So now I have a pen to remind me of another pen that reminded me of a friend, a friend whose face I can't even remember anymore. There have been other deaths in my life since then and they all hurt in their way, but not like that one. Too young, too early, too random.

Maybe it's better she gave the pen away. Another memory I don't need — leave it in the past, like a pen tucked away in a corner of my desk drawer where my wife won't be able to find it next time.

Well, maybe not too well-hidden, in case somebody needs to write something down.

LESSON 70

FOR WHERE YOUR TREASURE IS, THERE WILL YOUR HEART BE ALSO

LESSON

71

ANIMALS

My grandmother grew up on a number of farms. I suppose she saw a lot of animal cruelty there. And she was Chinese, and a woman, in Canada in the 1920s, so she experienced a lot of cruelty herself. And while she was not educated, she was clever and she put two and two together. She would always tell me that people who were cruel to animals would be cruel to people.

That is the one lesson I've been taught that I have observed to be 100% true throughout my life and I'll stand by it to my dying day. You abuse an animal, you're dead to me. And I will teach my kids this lesson and reinforce it over and over, because I know it to be true.

I married a woman who wouldn't even touch my old cat, but now pets and holds our new cat. And our kids love our cat, playing with him and hugging him and adoring him, all of which I'm unbelievably relieved to see. But my wife's mother, she hates cats.

She's actually terrified of them. She recoils in horror if the cat comes near. She taught her kids to hate cats too — luckily, I was able to get through to one of them and change her mind. I don't know what my mother-in-law would do if there were no consequences, but I'm sure she'd prefer if our cat — and all cats — were dead.

My cat, one of the sweetest cats I've ever known, who just wants to sit on warm laps or in sunbeams, who sleeps on my bed and whom I trust enough to let him wake me by poking his paws in my eyes.

So now, I have to make sure one of the most valuable lessons I know wins out over my mother-in-law's influence. Cats — plus all the other animals she hates and fears — against my mother-in-law. My kids turning out to be decent human beings vs. one of the most vile, poisonous, caustic people I've ever known, who treats people about as well as she treats cats.

Two different grandmothers, two different viewpoints, two different lessons. Thank goodness my kids are clever. They'll figure it out.

LESSON 71
BE KIND TO DUMB ANIMALS

72

GIFT

What kind of dad are you?

Maybe you're the kind of dad who builds his children a sandbox. That's cool — kids love sandboxes.

Maybe you're the kind of dad who hires somebody to build his kids a sandbox. You don't know how to do it yourself, but you want them to be happy. Nicely done.

Maybe you're the kind of dad who digs up part of the garden instead. Dirt, sand — what's the difference? Kids should get dirty. It's better for their immune systems. Good job.

Maybe you're the kind of dad who buys a bunch of cheap toys and buries them in the sandbox, little treasures for your kids to find. Very thoughtful.

Or maybe you're the kind of dad who goes to the butcher shop and gets the biggest animal bone he can. You bury it in the sandbox as deep as you think your kids can dig, then you sit back and wait for the screams of excitement. You stroll out to the garden where they have the bone half out of the hole.

"Oh, for the love of... Cover that thing back up. The smell will attract more. Took me over an hour to kill that one."

What kind of dad are you?

Or, more pointedly, what kind of dad am I?

LESSON 72

NEVER LOOK A GIFT HORSE IN THE MOUTH

LESSON

73

BETTER

I read somewhere that kids learn to tell time easier if you give them an analog clock instead of a digital one. It allows them to better see how an hour is broken up into sixty minutes and how much a half-hour is, or a quarter, and how seconds turn to minutes turn to hours. Digital may be easier to read, but analog gives a better fundamental understanding of our timekeeping system.

I couldn't agree more. But I think it goes deeper than that.

We learn to tell time in an attempt to master it, schedule it, control it, but we can't even stop it. Like the hands of an analog clock, it keeps spinning on, rising and falling in infinite loops. There is no better physical representation than an endless circle with no beginning or end.

A digital clock has no meaning, a jumble of numbers with no understanding of itself. If you would learn from that, you might as well learn to fly from a rock.

Time is a tricky thing. Sometimes it seems to pass so slowly, at other times you barely notice it sneaking up on you. One day, you think you have all the time in the world, then suddenly forty years have gone by and you haven't even started.

Time is a thief. It's also a liar, a coward, a trickster, a con.

Time is immutable, unmovable, unforgiving, and utterly heartless.

Time existed before anyone knew what time was, before there was anybody around to measure it. That we try is a joke and time can't be bothered to laugh.

Time is a cat burglar, a mugger, an uninvited houseguest who eats all your food. Time made you old, made you sick, made you fail, made you lose. Time made you lost. Time made and unmade you.

Time marches on, as do you, until you fall. But time keeps on going.

This is your new clock. It is a cartoon mouse. The short arm is the hour hand, the long arm is for minutes.

This is how you will learn to tell time. And you will learn nothing.

LESSON 73

BETTER LATE THAN NEVER

LESSON

74

RESPECT

What the hell are you doing? I'm busting my ass all day at work and I have to come home exhausted to *this?* Seriously, I just got in the door. Can't I get five minutes to catch my breath?

Well, what'd you go and do that for? Now I have to clean up your damn mess. Why can't you take care of it? Holy crap, it's not that complicated. Are you ever going to start thinking for yourself? Should I be worried when you do?

Why is it so hard for you? Why do I have to do everything around here? Can't you pick up some of the slack? What good are you?

Well, I don't want to shout at you. Do you think I enjoy this? Do you think I like getting all mad and worked up all the damn time? You certainly don't make it easy for me, that's for sure.

God, it's like you're *trying* to push my buttons. You know how stressed I am at work. Do you have to add to it? You're so aggravating. You need to stop this. Do you think you can do that?

What, no answer? You don't have anything to say? Are you just going to stand there with that dumb look on your face? Oh, for chrissakes, are you crying? Did I hurt your little feelings? Well, then, maybe you'll remember this and get things right next time.

Honestly, you brought this on yourself. You're the one to blame here. I'm not the one who screwed up. Well, I guess I did when I married y... oohhh, hi kids! Uh, it's okay, Mommy and Daddy were just having a little talk. Why don't you go to your rooms and we'll see you in a bit? Mommy's fine — she's just a bit upset, it's nothing. She's fine. Go to your rooms. Shut the door. Go on, now. Go.

LESSON 74
RESPECT OTHER PEOPLE'S PRIVACY

LESSON

75

DON'T

Lunchtime at my crappy, menial retail job! Time to go to the back room, chew on a granola bar, and ruminate on my life, what wrong turns I took to end up here. But first, bathroom break. It doesn't require all my concentration either. I can pee and feel bad about myself at the same time.

The third back aisle offers a clear path to the washrooms. The second is completely blocked off by skids of product. In the closest back aisle, a co-worker is manoeuvring a Skyjack back and forth, trying to get it as close as possible to the column so he can plug it in. It's a smaller model, but it still weighs several hundred pounds. He's about three feet off the ground and can't see what's immediately in front or behind him. For that reason, we don't like to use them during store hours, but if we do, we have someone act as a spotter. For whatever reason, he doesn't have one today. I could walk two aisles over, but I decide to wait the thirty seconds or so it'll take him to park it.

A small girl, maybe five or six years old, comes down the main aisle towards us.

She passes the third back aisle, then passes the second because of the blockage. As she gets to me, she sees the narrow opening between the Skyjack and the column and she dives in.

I can't say anything for a split-second. I'm too shocked.

"Stop! Stop! Stop!"

My co-worker's hands immediately come off the controls and the Skyjack stops. The girl stops too and turns to look at me quizzically. I can't think of anything to say, so I just wave her off. She continues on, completely oblivious to how close she came to being crushed to death. My co-worker looks down.

"Wow, that was close!" he chuckles.

I go to the bathroom, trying not to spray all over because I'm shaking so hard. I play it over and over in my head. What if I'd gone around, what if I hadn't waited, what if I hadn't been working that day? Maybe it was meant to be. If not a higher power, then fortuitous chance, a happy set of coincidences that led to that moment so I could be there for that girl. Every bad decision I ever made, every ill turn of Fate suddenly seemed like it was part of a bigger plan, guiding me to get there, to that exact spot at that exact time on that exact day.

Suddenly, I felt okay with my crappy, menial retail job, right up until I quit a few weeks later. After all, Fate didn't need me there anymore.

LESSON 75

Don't settle for less than you deserve

LESSON
76

MEEK

I wish I'd stood up for myself more when I was a kid. I wish I'd stood up for others, too. Instead, I let myself be cowed and bullied, pushed around, and taken advantage of by bigger kids, bolder kids, more forceful kids.

I was too easygoing, too complacent, too unwilling to put up a fight. Afraid of getting beat up, afraid of looking foolish, afraid of attracting attention.

And now I see it in my son. That meekness, that weakness, that "I'll let it go if you leave me alone." And it pains me. I don't want him to live like that, like I did.

So I tell him to stand his ground, don't take that crap, push back as hard as they push you. And he doesn't.

I forget he doesn't have my experience. He doesn't have my confidence. He doesn't know his limitations yet, let alone what he's capable of.

But I know he can do it. He can do what I didn't, he can be what I wasn't. He could fight injustice, protect his friends, and be able to look back on his life with pride, just like I would have if somebody had convinced me I could.

But still he doesn't. Because I forget he's just a little kid and the world is huge and scary and confusing. Because at his age, a bigger kid is a lot bigger. Because it's all too easy for me to project my adult sensibilities, my desires, my capabilities onto his tiny shoulders.

Almost as easy as hindsight.

LESSON 76
BLESSED ARE THE MEEK, FOR THEY SHALL INHERIT THE EARTH

77

AUTHORITY

Of all the stupid things my mother ever told me in my lifetime, I think the stupidest was "If it rains on your birthday, it means you're selfish."

I don't know where she got that from or what she was trying to accomplish, but all it did was stress me out about the weather in the week leading up to my birthday. It didn't make me any less selfish, just desperate to hide it. Except I couldn't, because I couldn't hide the weather.

If it happened to rain on somebody else's birthday, I'd smugly note the intensity of the downpour as an indicator of their selfishness and adjust my attitude towards them accordingly. But I'd spend my birthday in fear and dread if the sky was the least bit overcast. If any drops did fall, I'd tense up in anticipation of all my classmates rising up and taunting me: "Brad's selfish, Brad's selfish!"

But the taunts never came. Of course not.

I eventually figured out it was a load of crap. I lived in a city where it actually rained a lot, so people could just move somewhere sunnier if they didn't want anybody to know how selfish they were. But were sunny cities full of more generous people? Was my city perpetually wet because we brought it upon ourselves? Were our attitudes somehow affecting the weather?

I congratulated myself on outsmarting my mom and scoffed at how stupid and gullible I used to be.

Years later, I learned about climate change, global warming, and how the pollution we create affects weather systems. I realized she was somehow completely right about it while also being completely wrong. It's my new goal in life to accomplish that with my own children. Except I don't want to ruin their birthdays, so I'll just choose some other holiday at random. Perhaps if it rains on Valentine's Day, it means you're unloved. Seems plausible enough.

Years later, they'll tell me how I ruined Valentine's Day for them. I'll tell them how it could have been their birthdays and they'll thank me for it. Probably.

LESSON 77
QUESTION AUTHORITY

78

ALWAYS

I use reverse psychology on my son a lot. He's very shy and doesn't like trying new things, but he's also very defiant. He tests his boundaries with us all the time, seeing what he can get away with, standing up to us to see where the line is and if he can move it back.

So when I want him to do something I think he'd enjoy and he won't do it, then I tell him that he's not allowed to. I forbid him from doing it and I pretend to get a little mad. He squeals and runs away and does it to defy me — most of the time he ends up liking it.

I can totally see this backfiring on me in the future. I tell him not to do something, he does it anyway and it turns out to be fun, I was never really mad at him to begin with — yeah, that's not a good pattern to establish.

But I'm not sure how to change my approach. He sets his mind so firmly and won't do things I ask him to. Trickery is the only thing that's working right now. Do I switch tactics and dig in for a fight or enjoy this while it lasts?

Maybe I should confuse him by tricking him into doing something he really doesn't like once in a while. It would break up the pattern and I'd be blameless because I did tell him not to do it. But do I take the chance and betray his trust?

Perhaps I'll try that. I am trying to expand his horizons and introduce him to new things, after all.

LESSON 78
IF YOU DO WHAT YOU'VE ALWAYS DONE, YOU'LL BE WHO YOU'VE ALWAYS BEEN

LESSON

79

PRESENT

When do I stop feeling phony?
When do I feel like I'm doing this right?
Did I miss orientation?
It's like I became a dad just overnight.

My mother always seemed so certain
And she never questioned her authority.
If she had self-doubt, she never
Let it slip out. There was nothing to see.

My wife, she gets so frustrated.
Her parenting skills... I cannot do as well.
We have had kids for the same time.
If she is faking, I just cannot tell.

The neighbourhood parents are raising
Their kids their own way, but sometimes I see
Flaws that could come back to haunt them.
I wonder if they feel the same about me?

Perhaps I will feel I know something
When my kids are grown and they have kids, too.
For then, I will be a grandfather
And grandparents always know just what to do.

LESSON 79

THERE'S NO TIME LIKE THE PRESENT

LESSON

80

HAPPY

I 've been openly and unabashedly jaded and cynical for a long time, as long as I can remember. That really doesn't work when you have young kids, so I had to change. There's so much awe and wonder and joy in their little eyes and faces and voices, I feel like the biggest heel in the world if I have to suppress that just a little.

So I feign interest in every colourful rock they find. I fake excitement over every fuzzy animal they see. I ooh and aah at every anthill, firetruck, falling leaf, seashell, found coin, toy car, pine cone, and discarded coffee-cup lid they hold up to my face because I know they just want to share their excitement with me.

It's been hard, going against my inner nature, but it's been worth it. They're so fascinated by everything, it's truly inspiring to watch. Part of me wishes I could switch places with them so I could experience the world anew and marvel at its secrets and intricacies. But part of me can't wait until they're teenagers — moody, sullen, and snarky — so I can join them and go back to being my regular old self.

I'm pretty sure when that happens, I'm not going to be happy about it either. As uncomfortable as I am being so full of wonder and appreciation all the time, I kind of like it. It's as if I finally have permission to enjoy life. I'm seeing the world through their eyes and it's a lot of fun.

I'll be sad to see it go. Almost as sad as I'll be watching them turn into me.

LESSON 80

MOST FOLKS ARE ABOUT AS HAPPY AS THEY MAKE UP THEIR MINDS TO BE

LESSON

81

LOOK

O ur son fell down at the park the other day and bashed his chin. There was a bit of blood and some tears but he's fine now. You were worried he might get a permanent scar, but I'm not.

Little boys are supposed to get scars. They're trophies, markers, medals to show a day well fought and played. They tell the world you took a risk, got knocked down, and got up again. A boy without scars is a boy who did nothing.

Remember when we first met, when we knew something was happening and we lay in bed and you went over my body and examined all my scars? I had a story for each one. The leg scar from falling out of a treehouse. The elbow scar from the dirt-bike accident. The scuffed knuckles from a fight I sheepishly admitted I lost.

One day, that'll be our son. He'll meet somebody and they'll want to know all about him, his life, the story of his body. And he'll take them through it, a little roadmap of mini-dramas, and afterwards they'll feel they know him all the better for it.

They'll know he went out in the world, took a hit, and kept going. They'll know he's tougher than that, that it slowed him down, but it couldn't stop him. They'll know he tried.

We brought him in and cleaned him up and wiped off the blood and dirt, then he picked out a Band-Aid from the box and we put it on. If it doesn't scar, that's fine, it wasn't much of a story anyway. But if it does, that's fine too. Either way, we'll be back at the park tomorrow. Far be it for me to play the role of censor.

LESSON 81
LOOK BEFORE YOU LEAP

I knew this woman who was born in Thunder Bay, Ontario, and she grew up kind of poor but she was a good student and went to school and became a registered nurse, then she moved out to Vancouver and met a guy at a party and fell in love and got married and had two kids, but then he died when she was only 27 but she kept on going, because what else was she going to do, she had kids to look after and she never remarried because she worried another man might hurt her children, so she worked really hard to raise her kids on her own and one turned out pretty good but the other was kind of a dick and lazy and a loser who didn't really treat his mother as well as he should have but now he's finally got his shit together and even has a bit of money to take her out to dinner once in a while but he can't because life just keeps on going, you know, until it doesn't.

LESSON 82

STOP AND SMELL THE ROSES

83

MARK

I 'm standing in the gym, staring down my high school bully. Just like I should have done twenty years ago...

Back then, he must have outweighed me by at least fifty pounds. Impossibly broad shoulders, arms as big as my legs — of course he was on the football team. His nickname was 'Bruiser'. I couldn't expect any mercy, why should I expect originality?

He spots me from across the gym. A flicker of recognition, then a sly smile creeps over his face as he remembers me. I recognized him right away. As if I could ever forget that ugly mug.

I was smaller then. And a geek. I hugged the walls, doing my best not to be noticed, to get through the day without an extra test that wasn't in the official school curriculum.

I wasn't sure if I was going to go to the reunion. Not too many happy memories. Mostly of being scared and confused and worried a good deal of the time. I had friends, but they were geeks too, too afraid of getting picked on themselves to be of any help. It was nice to see them again, if only to remember why I don't keep in touch.

I've never been able to figure out exactly why I snapped. He wasn't picking on me extra hard that day. I wasn't particularly unhappy or stressed. And neither of us had realized just how much I had grown over the summer. I think it was partly the fact that I was graduating that year and felt that I finally deserved a little respect. I shouldn't be getting pushed around like some freshman kid. But mostly, I'd simply had enough.

A friend of mine had told me about going to his high school reunion and how delighted he was when he saw that his bully had gone completely bald. Mine wasn't bald and he was still mean-looking and ugly, but he didn't seem as large or imposing as he once did.

Thankfully, we had a substitute teacher that day, so I didn't even get in trouble. Bruiser kept leaning over and slapping me with a plastic ruler when the teacher's back was turned. I gritted my teeth — one more, just one more, just one more — and then it was too many.

He's moving in closer, sizing me up. I don't cower anymore, I don't run away. He tries to start circling me, but I refuse to turn. So he's forced to stop and now we're face-to-face. I level my cool stare at him, the one I've had twenty years to perfect.

I grabbed him off of his seat in a headlock, then brought my fist down on the top of his head. I'd never hit anybody before, so I didn't know that was a dumb move. *Ow*. His arms flailed about, trying to grab me. He should have covered his face.

A small crowd is watching us, pointing and whispering. Perhaps they remember that day. Probably not as vividly as I do, but some of them might have been there. And now they're hoping we'll finally have a rematch.

When people ask me if I had a favourite teacher, I always tell them, "Bruiser". And they ask me what he taught and I tell them that he taught me that deep down, all bullies are cowards. It was the best lesson I ever learned in high school, one I've used throughout my life ever since.

It's twenty years later. We're adults now. I wonder if he's got kids and if his kids are bullies too. I hope not. I hope he teaches his kids that you don't just go around punching people for fun or over petty grudges or to solve your problems. I hope I do. I've grown, both physically and emotionally. I'm confident, self-assured, and centred. And I notice that he still has a small scar on the bridge of his nose...

He never laid a hand on me again after that day.

I break out a huge smile and grasp his hand firmly in mine and shake it. I clap my other hand onto his shoulder and say, "Thanks again, Bruiser."

I turn on my heel and walk out of the gym, chuckling to myself. I don't look back. I don't have to.

LESSON 83
LEAVE YOUR MARK ON THE WORLD

LESSON

84

STRANGERS

I'm driving behind a Volvo station wagon with two little girls
sitting in the back. They're strapped in, facing me, and
they're waving, waving, waving. They're waving at everybody
and anybody — I just happen to be the one directly behind
them at the moment. And I know what this is, I know why
they're doing this. All they want is for somebody to wave back.
That's it. A simple wave in their direction would make them
happy. Maybe they're keeping track. Maybe it's a competition. I
wonder if anybody's waved at them today.

Whatever, I can't just do that.

I never waved at cars when I was a kid. I was too shy. I
wouldn't have known what to do if somebody had waved back,
acknowledged my existence. Probably slunk down in my seat,
ignored them, tried to be invisible.

The hard part now is driving safely while trying to look off
to the side so as not to make eye contact. They're still waving,
waving, waving as we stop at yet another red light. I'm still pretty
shy, but not as shy as I used to be. I take the opportunity to
fumble around for the hand puppet I keep in the pouch behind
my seat.

Still watching them while trying to look like I'm not, I slowly bring the puppet up beside me and wave its little paw at them. The reaction is immediate.

This is the greatest thing that has ever happened in the entire history of waving at people! Forget train engineers and firefighters, that's a freaking puppet! I can't hear them, but I see they're absolutely shrieking with delight. One of them twists around to tell the driver what's going on. Now they're waving even harder, waving with both hands, they're waving with their whole bodies. I don't know what else they think could happen, if this could somehow get better, the puppet's already doing a little dance — that's all I can do without running off the road.

I finally get an open lane, so I speed up to pass. I can't keep this up all afternoon. The girls contort in their seats to get one last wave in, while the puppet waves goodbye in kind, then returns to his pouch. Always leave them wanting more.

I want my kids to be friendly and not too shy. I want them to wave at people — and cars and trains and firetrucks and cops and construction workers and cyclists. And I want people to wave back.

That means you. Because that's my kid waving. Or, at least, I hope he is. If he's like I was, he's slinking down in his seat, trying not to get noticed, but he'll make up for it when he's older.

LESSON 84

DON'T TALK TO STRANGERS

LESSON

85

COMMITMENT

You probably have a local pizza place. It's close to your house, so it's convenient. They have a decent selection, it's not too expensive, and you've gotten to know some of the staff there. You might even have a regular pizza night once a week.

Then, one day, you go out with some friends and you're way across town and you all get hungry and somebody says they know a great pizza joint. So you go to a place you never would have gone to on your own, a pizza place that's so far out of the way you couldn't really justify going there again unless you happened to be in the neighbourhood, let alone once a week, and, *goddammit*, the pizza is incredible.

Seriously, it's amazing. The crust is perfectly chewy and crispy, the toppings are fresh, the place is clean, and the staff are super-friendly. It's so good, you can't believe the slop you've been eating at your local pizza place. It's so good, you wonder how your local can even justify calling theirs pizza. It's so good, your heart breaks a little as you leave, knowing you may never have that pizza again.

Then you're back home and pizza night rolls around again and you think of the best pizza you ever had. The crust, the toppings, how fantastic it was, but it's So. Far. Away.

And you call up your local, and you order your usual. You open the box and smell the familiar local smell and, just as you take that first bite, you think maybe it'll compare, maybe something changed, maybe it got just as good overnight somehow.

But it didn't. It's the same as always. Except it tastes a little worse now because of the comparison.

You sigh a little and shrink inside a bit. You think about how far away the other pizza place is and how you wish it were closer and more convenient. But you resign yourself to your local and you tell yourself that it's good enough.

That exact moment there, the moment of resignation — that's how I feel all the time.

That's the best I can explain it to you, at least in a way you might understand. If I could give you some advice, it would be to try as many different pizza places as you can before settling on one. If you're going to have just one pizza for the rest of your life, it should be the best one.

Now, I'm not saying your mom isn't the best, she is for you, just not for me. That's why I'm moving across town, so to speak. I need that crust, those toppings — sorry, the metaphor's getting a bit awkward and gross.

I don't expect your mom to understand. I don't expect you to understand either or to forgive me. At least, not until you've had a lot more pizza.

I'm sorry, son. Here's twenty bucks, next one's on me. Holy crap, this metaphor is terrible.

LESSON 85
Don't be afraid of commitment

LESSON

86

EVIL

I listen to the news on the radio in the car, sometimes with my son in the back seat. And, like usual, they talk about all the horrible things that are happening in the world.

I remember being my son's age and listening to the news on the radio in the car as my mom drove. And being terrified. An endless supply of shootings, stabbings, bombings, fires, death, destruction, and mayhem, sure to find us in our little suburban home one day.

I look back at my son sitting quietly in the back seat and wonder how much he understands.

Does he know what they're talking about? Does he understand the words, the concepts, the ideas, the conflicts? Is he scared? Will it give him nightmares? Does he know there is good in the world, so much more than the bad, that they'll never mention on the news on the radio in the car? Shouldn't he?

"What are... what are you thinking about?" I ask nervously.

"Cupcakes," he replies.

Okay then. We'll come back to that one later.

LESSON 86
SEE NO EVIL, HEAR NO EVIL, SPEAK NO EVIL

LESSON

87

LIFE

When I was younger, much younger, I vowed to myself to try something new every day. A new experience, a food I'd never eaten before, a place I hadn't visited yet. It didn't have to be something big each time, just enough to keep things interesting, offer some variety, shake things up, if only a little.

I remembered my vow years later with some amusement tinged with sadness. I couldn't fool myself into thinking I'd done everything I wanted to do, so instead I softly chuckled at that dumb kid with all the time, money, and opportunities he thought he'd have. Then I probably shut off the TV and collapsed into bed, exhausted after the day's work.

I remembered my vow again sometime after my first child was born. Babies need some sort of routine and we embraced that a little too fully. Breakfast, lunch, and dinner at set times consisting of foods we thought he'd eat, visiting the same child-friendly places over and over, certainly nothing spontaneous that didn't require planning, packing a bag, and extra wipes. I really couldn't blame him. I was too tired to be resentful anyway.

I remembered my vow again after our second child was born. By then, I figured the unpredictable nature of children would be the spice of life I thought I craved. Surely, cleaning different expelled fluids off of different pieces of furniture qualified.

I remembered my vow just the other day. My kids are older and demand new experiences daily. "I'm bored" is their mantra, coupled with expectant stare-downs. I'm trying my best, but I'm out of practice.

I want to tell them to slow down, pace themselves, they'll have the rest of their lives to try new things, but I know it's a lie. They're going to get old, they're going to get tired, they're going to fall into a rut and not know how to get out.

But I don't say anything because, years ago, I made a vow to myself to try new things every day. And I'm holding myself to it, even if sometimes those new things are just finding different ways to kid myself.

LESSON 87
WHEN LIFE GIVES YOU LEMONS, MAKE LEMONADE

88

YOURSELF

I used to be obsessed with how I smelled.

Bad breath, body odour, stinky feet — these were all legitimate worries, things that could drive other people, especially females, away.

Breath mints, deodorants, soaps and shampoos, powders and balms — I used them all, anything to stop the stink of me.

But it didn't work. The products did, but I remained alone. No one ever wanted to get close and stay close, even though I smelled pleasantly of mint and coconuts.

Turns out the problem was my personality. No one wants to be with someone who constantly puts others down, who always insults and mocks those he thinks are lesser than him, a smug, smirking asshole who uses sarcasm and indifference to keep everybody at arm's length.

All those years, I thought I stunk. I was right.

LESSON 88
BE YOURSELF

LESSON
89

LIVING

I think Young Me would hate Old Me.

I can look back at my young self with some amusement, click my tongue, and snicker at what an ignorant little shit I used to be. But if Young Me could see Old Me, what he was to become, I don't think he'd be so kind.

I used to stand for things. I had ideals, aspirations, integrity — there were passions in my life. I had opinions on things that mattered. I actually left the fucking house once in a while.

What did you become, old man? What did you do to me? You abandoned your principles. For what? A little bit of cash? You took a crappy job at a crappy company, selling your soul for a weekly pittance? You used to talk so big, but when it came down to it, you caved in, gave in, left it all behind? Is there even any trace of who you used to be left?

I know my son, Young Me, will one day look at me, Old Me, with some measure of contempt. Maybe he'll hate me, maybe he'll even say it and the words will cut, but they'll be justified.

And I'll just sadly smile at him and say, "Beat you to it."

LESSON 89
THE UNEXAMINED LIFE IS NOT WORTH LIVING

LESSON

90

STRONG

O ne of these days, you're going to fall in love. And when that's done with, you're going to fall in love again. And again, and again, and then hopefully one day you'll meet your soulmate.

I can't tell you how you'll know. You just will. Something about this other person will just click. It could be instant or it could take a while for you to realize it. Hopefully, it won't take long. And hopefully, they'll figure it out around the same time.

Don't make the mistake of thinking every person you fall in love with is your soulmate. Love can change over time — it adjusts and adapts, it flails and withers, it lies and deceives. When you meet your soulmate, *if* you meet your soulmate, there should be no doubt, no distrust, no dishonesty.

When you find them, it won't make sense. It'll just feel right, like all the other times, but more. There should be no second-guessing, no hesitation, no nagging at the back of your mind. The love won't fade, it'll grow and keep growing each day you're together. It'll survive any test, any hardship, any temptation you could throw at it.

But you still have to be so careful. Love is a trickster. It'll fool you and you'll follow it blindly. You'll think you've found your soulmate, but it was temporary — a stand-in, a placeholder.

And the thing is, you can't tell. You won't know if they're your soulmate until they're not.

I wish I could tell you how to know, but I can't. Because I don't know. It's something you'll have to learn and experience for yourself. Everybody in the world has to do it and you will too.

I know this, at least I know it now, because it happened to me too. I want you to love. I don't want you to get hurt, but you will and that's okay. You'll get your heart ripped out and it'll feel like the worst thing in the world, but you'll get over it. You'll be okay, just like I am.

Go on in, it's time. Is your mother okay? Say 'hi' to her for me. I'll see you next weekend.

LESSON 90

A CHAIN IS ONLY AS STRONG AS ITS WEAKEST LINK

LESSON
91

CONSIDER

I heard long ago that you should keep a journal. So I did, for a while, and then I stopped. I don't remember why.

I thought about it sometimes as an adult, whenever I would hear about other people re-reading theirs. The childish dreaming, the teenage drama, the vows and promises and long-abandoned goals, all funny and entertaining and mortifying and sad.

I often thought I should start again, but never did. The idea of recording my adult ramblings just didn't appeal. It would lack the innocence, the naïveté, and the vibrance of a child's take on the world, their life at the moment, and what the future might be or what they want it to be.

And then, one day, I found my old journal, mixed in with some of my mom's stuff when I was cleaning out her house. I recognized it immediately — the too-perfectly printed letters of a small child, the different shades of coloured pencil in an old-style lined-paper exercise book with my name neatly and proudly displayed across the cover. I sat down and opened it with eager hands.

Page after page of how much I hated everybody I knew. Every page, every entry, everybody.

I read it cover to cover, laughing at the pettiness of it, the ages-forgotten gripes and grudges, the childhood friends and acquaintances I hadn't thought of in years. Then, to my great regret, I threw it away.

I can't help but wonder — if I started a journal today, would it be any different? I hope so, but deep down, I'm pretty sure it wouldn't.

I will definitely encourage my kids to keep journals. They can record for posterity their dreams and goals, air their grievances, write terrible poetry, and one day in the far future, get a glimpse of who they were and who they were fated to become.

And if they don't like it, then they can just throw it away.

LESSON 91
CONSIDER THE PAST AND
YOU SHALL KNOW THE FUTURE

LESSON

92

SAY

My oldest won't talk to adults. He's just in preschool and he's fine with other kids, sometimes he's even the loudest kid in the room. But he won't talk to any adults outside of his family. Not his teachers, not his friends' parents, certainly not a friendly clerk in a store or a stranger. He won't answer direct questions, he won't ask for help, he'll barely say "thank you" and he needs to be prodded for that.

We're trying to get him to open up a bit, but in situations like this, when he can't or won't explain why he can't or won't do something, I try to remember back to when I was a kid and what I was like. Not that I was normal or anything hopeful like that, but he may have inherited more from me than a mere introverted nature and a receding hairline.

Then I remember, when I was a kid, I didn't talk to adults either and I remember exactly why: I didn't trust them.

Adults all had their own agenda and it almost never lined up with the kids'. But they were in control because they were bigger and that wasn't fair. And they were always talking about you, what was best for you, what you were going to have to do next, sometimes in front of you, but a lot of the time in hushed, conspiratorial tones when they thought you weren't listening or in another room with the door closed so they thought you couldn't hear.

And they lied! All the time! Kids get crap for lying, but adults get to do it constantly, with no repercussions. Big lies, small lies, lies to get you to do what they want, lies to get you out of their hair, lies to get you to shut up, lies for no apparent reason, at least not to a kid.

And what are you doing up there? Literally looking down at us, judging us, deciding our fates, pretending to know us and understand us and care. Like prison guards in a tower, like self-righteous demi-gods up on high, hurling your proclamations down upon us like lightning bolts of personal whims.

Why would I talk to you? Why would I give you any information? So you can use it against me? So you can think you're making progress and feel good about yourself? I ain't giving you shit.

So... I think I outgrew that. Mostly. Hard to tell.

I need to pull my kid aside and have a talk. The adults are concerned and we have to throw them off the trail. I want to tell him that a few shallow pleasantries can go a long way. Make some stupid small talk so they'll think you're normal, then they'll leave you alone.

But I don't want to tell him too much. I'm one of them now and sometimes I want him to do what I want, or to be quiet, for whatever reason I don't need to have. If I tell him all the secrets, then I'm giving up any advantage I might have over him.

All these years later, it's still us versus them. And this side of the battle is just as hard, probably more so. Nobody told me it would be like this, but then, I wasn't really talking to anybody.

LESSON 92
Do as i say, not as i do

LESSON

93

YESTERDAY

I went to a pawn shop today. I'd never been to one before. I once swore I'd never go to one. It wasn't a big deal after all. There are many things I vowed I'd never do. There aren't many of those left.

I once said I'd never deal with a real estate agent. When my dad was killed and it was announced on the radio the same day, a real estate agent phoned my mom to offer to sell her house for her because she probably wouldn't want to keep it now that her husband was dead. But here I am, four real estate agents later, all pleasant experiences.

I promised I'd never be civil to a lawyer. One of them took money to keep the man who killed my father out of jail on a technicality. Then, two of my new neighbours turn out to be lawyers, a really nice couple, thoughtful and sweet.

A funeral home worker tried so hard to upsell my mom on my dad's coffin. Then we buried my grandmother and they were so helpful and comforting.

Being part of an ethnic minority, I suppose I shouldn't have been so quick to judge entire groups of people based on the worst of those groups. I was just a kid, it got ingrained early, it was all I knew. You grow up, you experience more of the world, you change, the past slips away.

A man walked into a pawn shop and bought a gun, then used it to kill my dad.

I went to a pawn shop today. It wasn't a big deal.

But it kinda was.

LESSON 93

DON'T LET YESTERDAY USE UP TOO MUCH OF TODAY

94

BEGINNING

I never got a tattoo. I could never come up with a symbol or slogan that I thought I could stand behind for the rest of my life.

Even as a young man, I knew that my opinions and convictions were going to change as I got older, that the most important things in my life right now would be forgotten in a few years time.

You could argue that the fault was with me, that I couldn't be loyal to any ideal, TV show character, or brand of beer. But I could argue the opposite, that you only continue to espouse your outdated rhetoric/boy band because it's permanently inked on your bicep. I couldn't commit, but you were stubborn and refused to grow and mature.

I remember, as a kid, coming home with a temporary tattoo on my arm. My mother was so upset, she made me wash it off right away. My son came home with one once and I must have felt the same impulse. You fool, how could you mark your body like that, even in jest? Things are going to change, you're going to change, but a tattoo is for life.

Except it's not anymore. There's laser tattoo removal and it's gotten cheaper over the years. So even permanence isn't permanent anymore.

I could still get a tattoo, but I don't see the point. If you want one, fine, but I'll probably try to talk you out of it. It's not forever anymore, it's just inconvenient. The only thing I could ever commit to was not committing and there's no real symbol for that.

LESSON 94
KNOWING YOURSELF IS THE BEGINNING OF ALL WISDOM

LESSON
95

MORE

I don't listen to much new music anymore. I tend to listen to the music of my youth. There's that little jump of nostalgia attached to those old, familiar songs and that's what I seem to crave these days.

My son is starting to develop his own musical tastes. We don't have much overlap. He tends to skew quite definitely towards newer music.

I think all parents and kids are like this, it's not simply that he's weird or that I'm hopelessly outdated. It's like I can't help but be critical of his choices, as he is of mine, and it's a constant fight over the car stereo.

I hated my mom's music and she hated mine. I don't know how she felt about her parents' musical tastes or how my kids will feel about their kids', but I can guess how it'll go.

I suppose each generation has their own music, just like each generation has their own style, their own influences, their own way of doing things. Each generation expresses themselves differently, each generation rebels against the previous one.

At least, that's what my music told me. I'm not sure what my son's music is telling him — I can't stand to listen to that crap.

LESSON 95
THE MORE THINGS CHANGE, THE MORE THEY STAY THE SAME

96

EXAMPLE

I want my kids to be good people. I want my kids to care about others. I want them to have morals and ethics, to not be greedy or petty or mean.

I want my kids to be bold. I want them to explore, to take risks, and try new things. I want them to be cautious, I want them to travel and meet other people from different cultures, to make friends everywhere they go.

I want them to excel, I want them to make good decisions. I want them to be educated, knowledgeable, and wise. I want them to be productive, innovative, and to better the world through their efforts.

I want them to prosper. I want them to be generous. I want them to help others and not always put themselves first.

I want them to not care too much about things. I don't want them to live in the past and have regrets.

I want them to be polite and treat others with respect. I want them to stand up for themselves, for others, and against injustice. I want them to fight for what they believe is right. I want them to concede gracefully, if they must.

I want them to be spontaneous. I want them to be reliable. I want them to make others laugh.

I want them to be healthy. I want them to be well-rounded. I want them to enjoy themselves, to enjoy life, to the fullest extent possible. I want them to be happy.

I want my kids to be everything I'm not.

LESSON 96
LEAD BY EXAMPLE

LESSON
97

FORGIVENESS

Why is it so hard for you to say you're sorry?

You're clearly in the wrong here. You know that. You made a mistake, now you have to own up to it.

Every time you screw up, it's the same thing — you hope it'll disappear if you can just ignore it for long enough. You can get away with it sometimes, but not every time, certainly not this time.

It shouldn't be so difficult, but it is. As men, we're told to be strong, be confident, never back down, never show any weakness. These are the qualities we admire in our heroes, our movie stars, our politicians.

But what about when you really are wrong? Then, refusing to admit it is the true weakness. To be so stubborn and inflexible and unchanging in your position is to compile error upon error until everything is wrong and you just look a fool.

Be a man — a real man — and go to her. Tell her what you did. Don't tell her why. Don't make excuses. Don't blame her. Beg her forgiveness and tell her you'll never do it again. Look her in the eye, mean what you say, believe what you say, and hope she'll take you back. Not for her sake, not for the kids — for you.

I hope it works out. I hope she forgives me. I hope I get to be a husband again, and the parent my kids deserve, the parent I'm trying to be.

I know it's hard. Everything is so fucking hard. But if life was easy and nobody was ever wrong and nobody ever had to take responsibility and do the right thing and apologize, then nobody would need parents at all.

Thank goodness for our flaws. I love you so much.

And I'm sorry.

LESSON 97

IT'S EASIER TO GET FORGIVENESS THAN PERMISSION

98

SEE

I saw my old friend Bobby on the street, but I didn't say 'hi'. I recognized him right away. He looked different, yet still the same. I don't think he recognized me.

We used to be inseparable. He was always at my house or I was at his. We did everything together — toy cars, bikes, Lego, Star Wars, cops and robbers, kick the can, robots and outer space and cap guns. We were always going out to dinner with my mom or a movie with his parents or just hanging out reading comics. Always.

Then, suddenly, but somehow without noticing, it just ended. I was a year older and we made different friends at school. We stopped hanging out or talking, even though he lived just two doors down. We didn't even nod at each other when we passed in the hallways.

When he moved away, he didn't even say goodbye. All those years we'd spent together — I didn't necessarily want to keep in touch, but I felt that the fact that we'd shared so much at some point in our lives should have been acknowledged. But I didn't feel the sting long. Frankly, I didn't even notice he'd moved for a few weeks.

I don't know where he moved to, or what he did, or where he

went to school. I don't know what he does for a living, or if he's married, or if he has kids.

I don't know what he's like anymore. I don't know if he's happy, or well-off, or a good person. I don't know if he's the same kid I used to know or if he's changed.

Probably. I know I sure did. A long time ago.

LESSON 98
YOU MUST BE THE CHANGE YOU WISH TO SEE IN THE WORLD

LESSON
99

COMFORT

There's a picture on my wall of the Stanley Café in Thunder Bay, Ontario, taken sometime in the 1940s. It's the small diner my grandfather co-owned with some of his friends, where they worked and worked and worked so hard to scrabble together a living and care for their families. The picture is there to remind me of where I came from, how I got here, and of a hard life I don't want for myself.

My mom used to always say, "Stay in school and get your degree so you'll have something to fall back on." It was her dream that both her kids would finish university. So I studied and studied and studied so much, I burned myself out before I even got to university, where I struggled and flailed before dropping out. I was bored, I was lazy, there were other things I wanted to do, I had dreams of my own and I went after them with tepid enthusiasm and I threw my education away.

At the time, I couldn't see it, but I realize now that she was absolutely right. If I had gotten my degree, life would be so much easier. There are so many more jobs and opportunities that open up to you when you have your degree. Instead, I'm fumbling around, working crappy, unskilled, underpaid jobs, and just scraping by.

This isn't the life she wanted for me and it's certainly not the one I wanted for myself. But it's the one I chose, through apathy, stupidity, and neglect and I have to live with it.

To add insult to injury, it's only now that I understand what she was telling me. She wasn't saying to give up on my dreams at all. She wanted me to have a safety net, something to fall back on *in case* my dreams didn't pan out, didn't happen, or turned out to be less than financially lucrative.

Perhaps she had her own dreams for herself and they didn't work out, but she had her nursing degree. She fell in love, got married, and had kids, then when her husband got killed, she had something to fall back on.

I'm tired. I have another crappy, unfulfilling job. I barely remember my old dreams and sometimes even what it was like to have any.

My kids are getting their degrees. If I have to sit on them and force their faces into their books, they are getting their safety net. I've got my mom's arguments, I've got the stuff I figured out, I've got the picture of the Stanley Café.

But, perhaps most convincingly, I've got my piss-poor example of a life: "Stay in school and get your degree so you have something to fall back on and you don't end up like me."

I really hope it works. I really want them to be happy and successful. I want them to do better than I did, and my mother, and my grandfather, and not have to struggle and exhaust themselves just to get by. I want a better life for them, like my mother did for me and like my grandfather did for her.

That's my new dream, anyway.

LESSON 99

STEP OUTSIDE YOUR COMFORT ZONE

100

REPEAT

When I was very young, I decided that I would not only learn from my mistakes, I would also learn from everybody else's. This seemed to me to be the most efficient way to live a mistake-free life — to take the accumulated lessons of the world and use them as a guide to avoid repeating history unnecessarily.

So I held back and I watched and I listened and observed and I let other people make their mistakes, then I didn't do what they did. I avoided many of the problems and pitfalls that other people found themselves in — the inconveniences, the disasters, the pains and regrets.

Then I realized that I wasn't having any of the experiences that went along with the mistakes. I was learning the lessons, but I wasn't having any fun. I was missing out, not accumulating any stories of my own.

So I ventured out into the world and started having experiences of my own. Then, when I started making mistakes of my own, I tried to remember what others had done. But the lessons I'd learned from them were shallow and insubstantial because they weren't my own, so I forgot them and I ended up making the mistakes anyway. It took a while and there was a lot of repetition, but now you wouldn't know me from any other regretful idiot out there.

Except, of course, for me, there was that one mistake I made that was much bigger, if less obvious, than all the rest.

LESSON 100

THOSE WHO DO NOT LEARN HISTORY ARE DOOMED TO REPEAT IT

101

TIME

After all these years, I've finally got him, tied to a chair in his own house. I lay all my tools out on the floor in front of him, telling him what each one is for, what it's going to do to him. Then I get to work, taking slices and chunks from him, trying to cause as much pain as possible, revenge for all the pain he caused me, my mother, my family.

Or maybe I just pop up from a hiding spot and shoot him once in the heart, then set the place on fire, like he did to my dad. Perhaps not as satisfying, but more befitting. When the police fail you, when the courts fail you, somebody has to set things right. Justice must prevail, that's the way it's supposed to be.

It would have to happen on a significant date. My 18th birthday. My 21st birthday. 20 years to the day. 25 years to the day. It would take some planning, training, and luck to get this right, but it's okay, I've had years to prepare.

But it never happened. The milestones came and went. I thought about it so often over the years, fantasized about it, steeled myself in my head to spill blood, exact pain, take a life. I knew where he lived, not too far away, he'd be easy to find, easy to kill. But I never went through with it.

It's not that I didn't want to, it's not like I was afraid or I didn't know how. It's easy to take a life. Go to a store, buy a gun, pull a tiny little trigger, and a life ends. It's the aftermath that's hard to deal with.

A funeral to plan for a family torn apart. A stream of sympathizers, onlookers, gawkers, and gossipers. A young woman loses the love of her life, her children now half-orphaned. Court dates and police visits and that one day a year you have to be extra nice to Mom because she's on the verge of tears all day. Fear and despair and regret and remorse, depression and loneliness, anger and rage.

Someone once told me I wasn't a man because I never avenged my father's death. People, especially stupid people like that one, who don't know death or violence except from the movies, should perhaps shut the fuck up.

I didn't kill my father's murderer simply because my mother asked me not to.

I complain about her a lot, the peculiarities of how she raised me, her quirks and oddities and wrong ideas, but she's smarter than I am. She knew the path of revenge is ultimately a self-destructive one. She knew what I wanted to do — she must have known — like she knew I'd never get away with it, that it would end with me dead or in jail. And she knew that if that happened, it would probably break her. If anything could break my mom, the strongest person I've ever known, widowed at 27 with a young child and pregnant with a second, that would be it.

I've tried to kid myself over the years, fool myself into thinking I'm a good person, that I could never do what he did, but I think I could. But I'm glad I didn't.

Instead, I got to live a life. I grew up a free man, free to succeed or screw things up on my own terms. Free to get a series of crappy jobs, to fall in love, accumulate too much debt, and go for long walks to clear my head. Free to grow old and grow fat and watch too much TV and sleep in on weekends. Free to hang out at the mall and learn how to drive and travel up the coast and cook Thai food. Free to wreck my car and lose my hat and fall on my ass and get back up again, always get back up again, and adopt a cat and eat ice cream from the carton and sit on the deck and hold hands and finally, *finally*, let go of all the anger.

I'll never love him, I'm not that big. I'll never forgive him. But I can forget him. It's easy. Surprisingly so.

You'll have to excuse me, I have to go now. My kids will be home from school soon. Only a few hours until bedtime — gotta make the most of it.

LESSON 101
YOU'LL HAVE TIME

Sources

0 IT'S THE THOUGHT THAT COUNTS

This common phrase was originally "It is not the gift, but the thought that counts," written by Henry van Dyke, a second-generation clergyman who was also a professor of English literature.

1 BE CURIOUS ABOUT THE WORLD AROUND YOU

Kind of the opposite of "curiosity killed the cat", but how many books have cats written?

2 STRIVE TO BE A BETTER PERSON

Source unknown, but surely it's embroidered on more than a few pillows.

3 NOTHING IS MORE IMPORTANT THAN A GOOD EDUCATION

Roy Wilkins recalls his aunt telling him this when he started first grade in an otherwise all-white school. His father advised him that "no one can ever steal an education away from a man." He got his degree in sociology, eventually became the head of the NAACP during the Civil Rights Movement, and was awarded the Presidential Medal of Freedom by Lyndon Johnson.

4 DON'T TAKE UNNECESSARY RISKS

Likely, a lot of people said this but were lost to history, unlike those they were warning.

5 THE LEOPARD DOES NOT CHANGE HIS SPOTS

This is a colloquial version of a Bible verse, Jeremiah 13:23, the King James Version being "Can an Ethiopian change his skin or the leopard his spots?" Updating it for a more enlightened audience, the Contemporary English Version, revises it to "Can people change the colour of their skin, or can a leopard remove its spots?" So perhaps the answer is 'yes'.

6 THE FREE MARKET DICTATES VALUE

Surely if any one person had come up with this, they'd be rich and famous and we'd all know who it was.

7 THE SQUEAKY WHEEL GETS THE GREASE

Josh Billings wrote in his 1910 poem, "The Kicker":

I hate to be a kicker,
I always long for peace,
But the wheel that squeaks the loudest,
Is the one that gets the grease.

Or maybe he didn't. The poem in question gets other attributions and no definitive source has been established. The 1937 edition of *Bartlett's Familiar Quotations* credits Billings under his given name, Henry Wheeler Shaw. Whoever came up with the phrase in English might have been inspired by a proverb in German that translates as "The wheel that squeaks the loudest gets most of the fat."

8 MODERATION IN ALL THINGS

Hesiod's poem "Works and Days" asked

us to "Observe due measure, moderation is best in all things." In Euripides' play *Medea*, he references "Moderation, the noblest gift of heaven". Plato's *Gorgias* warned "We should pursue and practice moderation." Essentially, ancient Greeks wouldn't stop going on about moderation.

Johann David Wyss' *Swiss Family Robinson*, as translated by William H.G. Kingston, later gave us "moderation in all things." In similar fashion to the Greeks, Wyss doesn't stop at telling us this just once. To illustrate how good he was at following his own advice, the book was edited by his son Johann Rudolf and illustrated by his son Johann Emmanuel.

9 PUT SOME MONEY ASIDE FOR A RAINY DAY

Old advice from *The Bugbears* in 1580, probably authored by John Jeffere — "Wold he haue me kepe nothing against a raynye day?"

10 ALL'S FAIR IN LOVE AND WAR

John Lyly's 1579 *Euphues: The Anatomy of Wit* told us "the rules of fair play do not apply in love and war". Francis Edward Smedley apparently loved the sentiment — his *Frank Fairleigh*, published in 1850, noted "all is fair in love and war."

11 THERE IS A TIME TO GROW UP AND LEAVE CHILDISH THINGS BEHIND

There are various contemporary versions of this, adapted from 1 Corinthians 13:11. The King James Version has it as "When I was a child, I spake as a child, I understood as a child, I thought as a child: but when I became a man, I put away childish things."

12 SPEAK YOUR MIND

If any one person deserves credit for this phrase, they failed to say so loud enough to be noticed.

13 IF YOU WANT SOMETHING DONE RIGHT, DO IT YOURSELF

Charles-Guillaume Étienne wrote in *Bruis et Palaprat*, "On n'est jamais servi si bien que par soi-même." A direct translation into English would be "One is never served so well as by oneself." A prolific playwright, he was notably accused of plagiarism for his comedy *Les Deux Gendres*.

14 DREAM BIG

It's possible whoever came up with this phrase is known for some of their longer sayings, but they got no credit for this one.

15 TO BELIEVE IN SOMETHING, AND NOT TO LIVE IT, IS DISHONEST

Often attributed to Mohandas 'Mahatma' Gandhi, the earliest recorded version of this is in *The Internet Marketing Digest* from 2001, as an epigraph under the chapter title "How To Make Free Money From Your Website", where it is attributed to "M.K. Ghandi" — yes, not only did the author misspell the Mahatma's name, but it looks like he made up a quote about honesty and attributed it to him.

16 NO TREATS BEFORE DINNER

Isn't life hard enough already?

17 NEVER LEAVE THAT 'TIL TOMORROW WHICH YOU CAN DO TODAY

Advice from Benjamin Franklin's inaugural *Poor Richard's Almanac* in 1733. Good suggestion — that guy got a lot of stuff done.

18 HE THAT HATH NO CHILDREN DOTH BRING THEM UP WELL

One of many, many old English proverbs. Another, if less long-lived, offers its corollary: "He that hath children, all his morsels are not his own." Perhaps Eleanor Roosevelt summed it all up with "You'll be damned if you do and damned if you don't."

19 CLEAN YOUR ROOM

Every mom ever.

20 THOSE WHO CAN, DO. THOSE WHO CAN'T, TEACH.

George Bernard Shaw wrote this in *Maxims for Revolutionists*. He also used the phrase in his play *Man and Superman*.

21 IMITATION IS THE SINCEREST FORM OF FLATTERY

Charles Caleb Colton coined this phrase in 1820, with Oscar Wilde suggesting he add "that mediocrity can pay to greatness," which may explain why he's often credited as the source. Eustace Budgell had previously written "Imitation is a kind of artless flattery" in *The Spectator* in 1714. Prior to that, in their 1708 biography, *The Emperor Marcus Antoninus: His Conversation with Himself*, Jeremy Collier and André

Dacier wrote "You should consider that Imitation is the most acceptable part of Worship, and that the Gods had much rather Mankind should Resemble, than Flatter them."

We can presume they'd all be flattered.

22 BE PROUD OF WHERE YOU COME FROM

Somehow, it never occurred to whoever coined this phrase to leave a record of doing so.

23 DON'T JUDGE A BOOK BY ITS COVER

This proverb would seem too apologetic for anyone to claim authoring it in their own book.

24 IF YOU CAN'T SAY SOMETHIN' NICE, DON'T SAY NOTHIN' AT ALL

This may well have an earlier source, but we all know it from Disney's *Bambi*.

25 IT'S WEIRD NOT TO BE WEIRD

This is one of those few odd quotes regularly cited online that actually seems to be from the person it's attributed to, John Lennon.

26 KEEP YOUR SECRETS SAFE

Sara Shepard wrote "The only way to keep your secrets safe is to have none at all" in the 11th book in the Pretty Little Liars series, *Stunning*. That can't possibly be where this sentiment originated, but no prior source seems to be established.

27 IF YOU WANT THE RAINBOW, YOU GOTTA PUT UP WITH THE RAIN

Dolly Parton coined this one, with "The

way I see it" preceding it.

28 A ROLLING STONE GATHERS NO MOSS

Publilius (often rendered as 'Publius') Syrus wrote this as "Saxum volutum non obducitur musco" in his *Sententiae*. A Syrian brought to Italy as a slave, he gained his freedom out of respect for his wit and talents.

The 16th Century saw variations from Desiderius Erasmus and John Heywood.

The maxim inspired the Muddy Waters song "Rollin' Stone", which in turn was the inspiration for the name of the Rolling Stones. On an unrelated note, Bob Dylan's "Like A Rolling Stone" topped the list of "500 Greatest Songs of All Time" published by *Rolling Stone* in 2004 and has been covered by the Rolling Stones. Magazine founder Jann Wenner also cites the Muddy Waters song as inspiration for its title.

29 IT'S NICE TO BE IMPORTANT, BUT IT'S MORE IMPORTANT TO BE NICE

Famed journalist Walter Winchell gets the credit for this one, but in the parlance of the times, originated it by signing off one of his columns with "Your New York Correspondent, who wishes to remind celebrities that it is swell to be important — but more important to be swell!"

Others used the phrase, claiming credit or attributing it to people other than Winchell, with 'nice' eventually replacing 'swell'.

30 ACTIONS SPEAK LOUDER THAN WORDS

This proverb sprang from the 17th Century US in its current form, but exists in many languages, back to ancient Greek.

31 NOTHING GOLD CAN STAY

This is the closing line of Robert Frost's abiding poem of the same name.

32 WATCH YOUR STEP

This is one where it would be putting a foot wrong to attribute it to a single author.

33 ROCK THE BOAT

This dates back to the early 20th Century in its common phrasing, but it took the Hues Corporation to turn it into a disco song.

34 GET INVOLVED

This phrase can be an activist sentiment, suggest an unwanted onus that comes with something (generally when used in the negative: "I don't want to get involved"), or mean beginning a romantic relationship. A proverb collection edited by a German suggests it's American in origin, while other sources note the idiom originating in the UK.

35 YOU'RE NEVER TOO OLD TO LEARN SOMETHING NEW

Today, I learned that American author Suzy Kassem said this.

36 YOU CAN'T TEACH AN OLD DOG NEW TRICKS

This proverb is likely of English provenance. Dorothy Parker famously quipped that "You can't teach an old dogma new tricks," that variation appearing in a 1928 issue of *Life*.

37 OLD FRIENDS ARE BEST

English scholar and jurist John Selden coined this phrase in his *Table Talk*, which didn't see publication until fifteen years after his death.

38 LITTLE SAID IS SOONEST MENDED

This first appeared in George Wither's *The Shepherd's Hunting* in 1615. Wither was an English satirist known for a deliberately plain style, prompting the observation by Dame C.V. Wedgwood that "every so often in the barren acres of his verse is a stretch enlivened by real wit and observation." Wedgwood must have skipped this one.

39 CHILDREN SHOULD BE SEEN AND NOT HEARD

This old English proverb was originally aimed only at girls, appearing in John Mirk's *Mirk's Festial* in the middle of the 15th Century as "A mayde schuld be seen, but not herd." To be fair, 'mayde' was also used for celibate men, but the intended meaning was likely aimed at children just as it is today.

40 THE REWARD OF A THING WELL DONE IS TO HAVE DONE IT

Ralph Waldo Emerson generally gets the credit for this one, as it's found in his *Essays: Second Series*. However, his *Journals and Miscellaneous Notebooks* credits it to Seneca. It shouldn't really matter who gets the nod here, considering.

41 CHARACTER IS HABIT LONG CONTINUED

Plutarch coined this in *Moralia*, a collection of lectures, letters, and dialogues. Elsewhere in the same text, he also noted that "Character is destiny," which seems to counter the idea of choice set forward in the other saying.

42 AS YOU SOW, SO SHALL YOU REAP

This adage originates from the Bible, specifically Galatians 6:7. The King James Version renders it as "for whatsoever a man soweth, that shall he also reap".

43 IT IS BETTER TO FAIL IN ORIGINALITY THAN TO SUCCEED IN IMITATION

Herman Melville noted this in "Hawthorne and His Mosses", an essay reviewing Nathaniel Hawthorne's *Mosses from an Old Manse* four years after its publication. The essay was written while taking a break from writing *Moby Dick*.

44 HE WHO HESITATES IS LOST

English poet and essayist Joseph Addison coined this phrase in *Cato, a Tragedy*. This play touched on numerous themes, including republicanism versus monarchy, leading a number of scholars to cite it as the true source of various famous quotations from the American Revolution, including "I only regret that I have but one life to give for my country" and "Give me liberty or give me death!"

45 NOTHING MATTERS VERY MUCH AND FEW THINGS MATTER AT ALL

Among other things, Arthur Balfour was the Prime Minister of the United Kingdom from 1902–1905. Just the kind of thing you want to hear from your leader.

46 INTO EACH LIFE, SOME RAIN MUST FALL

Henry Wadsworth Longfellow coined this phrase in his poem "The Rainy Day".

47 SPARE THE ROD AND SPOIL THE CHILD

The poem "Hudibras", Samuel Butler's 1662 satire on the English Civil War contained these lines:

Love is a Boy,
by Poets styl'd,
Then Spare the Rod,
and spill the Child.

The intent seems the opposite of our current usage, imploring the reader to spare the rod. Butler, however, was likely responding to earlier versions of the phrase such as "Who-so spareth ye sprynge, spilleth his children" from William Langland's seminal 1377 poem *William's Vision of Piers Plowman*.

Langland's version pre-dates biblical versions written akin to our current phrasing, but the idea appears in Proverbs 13:24. The King James Version, first printed in 1611, renders that passage as "He that spareth his rod hateth his son: but he that loveth him chasteneth him betimes."

48 ALL ART IS QUITE USELESS

A pithy quote from the pen of Oscar Wilde, the context to this one is rather ironic — intentionally so, considering it appears in the preface to *The Picture of Dorian Gray*.

49 NO PRESSURE, NO DIAMONDS

This epigram is owed to Scottish philosopher, satirist, historian, and mathematician Thomas Carlyle. He also coined the phrase "the dismal science" to describe economics, his two-volume *The French Revolution: A History* inspired Charles Dickens' *A Tale of Two Cities*, his ideas were discussed in the development of both Socialism and Fascism, and his Carlyle circle is standardly used in working with quadratic equations. A hard act to follow.

Samuel Butler was glad Carlyle gave Jane Welsh a diamond, saying that "It was very good of God to let Carlyle and Mrs. Carlyle marry one another, and so make only two people miserable and not four."

50 ALL'S WELL THAT ENDS WELL

This is the title of one of William Shakespeare's 'problem plays', meaning that scholars cannot agree on whether it's a comedy or tragedy.

51 ALL GOOD THINGS MUST COME TO AN END

Geoffrey Chaucer penned this in *Troilus and Criseyde*.

52 IT TAKES ONE TO KNOW ONE

If I knew who originally said this, then I would be 'one', right?

53 HE WHO DARES, WINS

"Who Dares Wins" is the motto of the British Special Air Service, usually credited to its founder, Sir David Stirling.

54 BEGINNING IS EASY; CONTINUING, HARD

A Japanese proverb with a weird take on inertia.

55 ONLY THE MEDIOCRE ARE ALWAYS AT THEIR BEST

French dramatist and diplomat Jean Giraudoux wrote this phrase, but similar sentiments were put forward by W. Somerset Maugham ("Only a mediocre person is always at his best.") and Max Beerbohm ("Only mediocrity can be trusted to be always at its best.").

56 YOU ARE THE SUM OF YOUR MEMORIES

I knew who said this, but I forgot to write it down.

57 SECOND PLACE IS JUST THE FIRST LOSER

Coined by NASCAR racing legend Dale Earnhardt Sr., who would have made a terrible kindergarten teacher.

58 MIND YOUR OWN BUSINESS

Many credit this phrase as having a biblical origin, owing to St. Paul's advice in 1 Thessalonians 4:11, rendered in the King James Version as "And that ye study to be quiet, and to do your own business, and to work with your own hands, as we commanded you", but there's little support for a direct linkage. "Mind your beeswax" was a slang variant that came up in the 1930s. The acronym 'MYOB' dates back to 1962 and British science fiction author Eric Frank Russell's novella *...And Then There Were None*, which he later adapted into the latter section of *The Great Explosion*.

59 IT'S ALL RIGHT TO CRY

The sentiment would pre-date the song but Rosey Grier sang the Carol Hall-penned song of this name as part of

"Free To Be... You and Me", a children's entertainment project spearheaded by Marlo Thomas in 1972 after she was unable to find suitable books for her young niece to read.

60 BE A MAN

A sentiment echoed by insecure asshole dads everywhere.

61 THE MAN WHO MAKES NO MISTAKES DOES NOT USUALLY MAKE ANYTHING

Edward Phelps said this in a speech at the Mansion House in London, attributing it to Bishop W.C. Magee of Peterborough.

62 VIOLENCE BEGETS VIOLENCE

Popularly attributed to Martin Luther King Jr., the phrase has been used since at least the 1830s.

63 YOU MAKE YOUR OWN LUCK

Ernest Hemingway's son Gregory attributes this to his father in his book, *Papa, a Personal Memoir*.

64 DON'T COUNT YOUR CHICKENS BEFORE THEY HATCH

Aesop used this as the moral of his fable "The Milkmaid and Her Pail". None of Aesop's actual writings survived and we can't be sure he actually existed, but stories credited to him were gathered and compiled over time.

65 IT'S HARD TO BEAT A PERSON WHO NEVER GIVES UP

Babe Ruth coined this phrase in a 1940 article for *The Rotarian*, the magazine of Rotary International, as "You just can't beat the person who never gives up."

66 THESE ARE THE GOOD OLD DAYS

It seems sometimes that the number of possible sources for this quote is far outweighed by the number of people who disagree with its sentiment.

67 A LITTLE HARD WORK NEVER HURT ANYBODY

Source unknown, but probably somebody trying to get someone else to do something they didn't want to do.

68 PRESERVE YOUR MEMORIES, THEY'RE ALL THAT'S LEFT YOU

This line is from the title track of the Simon and Garfunkel album *Bookends*. The song appropriately appeared twice, both opening and closing side 1 of the record.

69 DO UNTO OTHERS AS YOU WOULD HAVE THEM DO UNTO YOU

This is the common English phrasing of Matthew 7:12, commonly known as 'The Golden Rule'. This is distinct from all common Bible versions, with the King James Version rendering it as "Therefore all things whatsoever ye would that men should do to you, do ye even so to them".

Similar sentiments exist in numerous traditions, suggesting a universal desire for ambiguity.

70 FOR WHERE YOUR TREASURE IS, THERE WILL YOUR HEART BE ALSO

This is another Bible quote, from Matthew 6:21. Notably, the phrasing remains the same in multiple common versions.

71 BE KIND TO DUMB ANIMALS

To whomever first said this, you could start by not calling them 'dumb'.

72 NEVER LOOK A GIFT HORSE IN THE MOUTH

This English proverb appeared in John Heywood's *A dialogue conteinyng the nomber in effect of all the prouerbes in the Englishe tongue* as "No man ought to looke a geuen hors in the mouth." This may have originated from the commentary on The Letter to the Ephesians by St. Jerome, which offers "Noli equi dentes inspicere donati" or "Never inspect the teeth of a given horse." All versions may be references to the Trojan Horse, noted in Virgil's *Aeneid* and Homer's *Odyssey*, in which case this is terrible advice.

73 BETTER LATE THAN NEVER

In "The Yeoman's Tale", part of his *Canterbury Tales*, Geoffrey Chaucer wrote "For better than never is late; never to succeed would be too long a period." However, the phrase in question is much older, used by Titus Livius in his *History of Rome* in 27 BCE as "potiusque sero quam nunquam."

74 RESPECT OTHER PEOPLE'S PRIVACY

Said by every parent of young kids without a lock on the bathroom door.

75 DON'T SETTLE FOR LESS THAN YOU DESERVE

If you're not going to at least write it down somewhere we can find it, then you don't get the credit for it.

76 BLESSED ARE THE MEEK, FOR THEY SHALL INHERIT THE EARTH

This is one of the Beatitudes from Matthew 5:5 in the King James Version of the Bible.

77 QUESTION AUTHORITY

As a familiar slogan, this phrase was popularized by Timothy Leary. However, some attribute the original sentiment to Socrates, who was put on trial for doing just that.

78 IF YOU DO WHAT YOU'VE ALWAYS DONE, YOU'LL BE WHO YOU'VE ALWAYS BEEN

A 1981 article in *The Milwaukee Sentinel* quoted family relationships and human sexuality counselor Jessie Potter as saying "If you always do what you've always done, you always get what you've always gotten" in her opening speech for the seventh annual Woman to Woman conference.

79 THERE'S NO TIME LIKE THE PRESENT

This adage was first recorded in 1562. John Trusler expanded it in his 1790 *Proverbs Exemplified*: "No time like the present, a thousand unforeseen circumstances may interrupt you at a future time."

80 MOST FOLKS ARE ABOUT AS HAPPY AS THEY MAKE UP THEIR MINDS TO BE

This phrase has been attributed to Abraham Lincoln by numerous sources, including various compilations of the man's sayings, countless online attributions, and the 1960 film *Pollyanna*.

The earliest source seems to be a January 1st, 1914 newspaper column by Dr. Frank Crane in which he discusses New Year's resolutions and exhorts readers to "Remember Lincoln's saying that 'folks are usually about as happy as they make up their minds to be.' "

However, Crane later cites the quote again in a 1916 column titled "Plain Talk for Plain People", but changing the phrasing from "folks" to "most people" and adding "in this world". In 1920, he offered a third version, all of which casts doubt on the authenticity of his attribution.

81 LOOK BEFORE YOU LEAP

This proverb of English provenance was noted in John Heywood's 1546 collection titled *A dialogue conteinyng the nomber in effect of all the prouerbes in the Englishe tongue*.

82 STOP AND SMELL THE ROSES

All that can be confirmed about this saying is that it's of North American origin. There are too many possible sources to be sure who said this first and it would be wrong to pick just one.

83 LEAVE YOUR MARK ON THE WORLD

A good way to do this is to come up with a memorable quote, then make sure it's attributed to you properly.

84 DON'T TALK TO STRANGERS

Who knows how many lives McGruff the Crime Dog saved?

85 DON'T BE AFRAID OF COMMITMENT
Says the divorced dad.

86 SEE NO EVIL, HEAR NO EVIL, SPEAK NO EVIL
This Japanese proverb was carved into the outer face of Sacred Stable in the city of Nikko, a UNESCO World Heritage Site, as part of a celebrated Shinto shrine. The famed image of Mizaru, Kikazaru, and Iwazaru, the three monkeys representing the proverb, is likewise carved there, though the words were lost to time. The monkeys' names are themselves a play on words which approximates the familiar wording.

Though the monkeys have been represented there since the 17th Century, they were originally introduced to Japan by a Chinese Buddhist monk. Rather than avoiding evil, the monkeys were following the orders of the fearsome god Vadjra in the earlier tradition.

87 WHEN LIFE GIVES YOU LEMONS, MAKE LEMONADE
Christian anarchist writer Elbert Hubbard coined this in his 1915 obituary of dwarf actor Marshall Pinckney Wilder as "He picked up the lemons that Fate had sent him and started a lemonade-stand."

Dale Carnegie gave credit to Julius Rosenwald for the phrase after using it in his 1948 book *How to Stop Worrying and Start Living* as "If You Have a Lemon, Make a Lemonade."

88 BE YOURSELF
Don't know who said this, but probably not an actor.

89 THE UNEXAMINED LIFE IS NOT WORTH LIVING
Plato's *Apology* depicts Socrates saying this during his trial for impiety and corruption of youth, for which he was sentenced to death.

90 A CHAIN IS ONLY AS STRONG AS ITS WEAKEST LINK
Thomas Reid's 1786 *Essays on the Intellectual Powers of Man* coined this phrase as "In every chain of reasoning, the evidence of the last conclusion can be no greater than that of the weakest link of the chain, whatever may be the strength of the rest."

91 CONSIDER THE PAST AND YOU SHALL KNOW THE FUTURE
Confucius is often credited with this one in its many variants. Either he couldn't foresee a future where nobody was sure whether he actually said it or he knew but didn't record it accurately anywhere, just to mess with us.

92 DO AS I SAY, NOT AS I DO
The disdainful context of this phrase is often lost in common usage. Appearing in John Selden's 1654 *Table Talk*, the full quote is "Preachers say, 'Do as I say, not as I do.'"

93 DON'T LET YESTERDAY USE UP TOO MUCH OF TODAY
Will Rogers was a seemingly endless repository of good advice and this certainly sounds like something he'd say. We can't be sure he actually said it, but we're not going to dwell on it too much.

94 KNOWING YOURSELF IS THE BEGINNING OF ALL WISDOM

This could be from Aristotle, but we just don't know. You know who *would* know? Aristotle.

95 THE MORE THINGS CHANGE, THE MORE THEY STAY THE SAME

This epigram from Jean-Baptiste Alphonse Karr was coined in French as "Plus ça change, plus c'est la même chose."

96 LEAD BY EXAMPLE

Too many people have said this and not lived up to it.

97 IT'S EASIER TO GET FORGIVENESS THAN PERMISSION

US Naval officer Grace Hopper was quoted as saying "It's easier to ask forgiveness than it is to get permission" in the US Navy magazine *Chips Ahoy!* However, earlier iterations date back to 1846, when Agnes Strickland's *Lives of the Queens of England* used the phrase "it being less difficult to obtain forgiveness for it after it was done, than permission for doing it."

98 YOU MUST BE THE CHANGE YOU WISH TO SEE IN THE WORLD

Educator Arleen Lorrance wrote in her book *The Love Project* that "One way to start a preventative program is to be the change you want to see happen." This stands as the earliest recorded source of the phrase, in 1974, long after the 1948 death of Mohandas 'Mahatma' Gandhi, to whom it is often attributed. Lorrance claimed to have 'received' this principle, and five others, while teaching at a high school in Brooklyn. As one of her 'Love Principles', she framed the advice as "Be the change you want to see happen, instead of trying to change anyone else."

In the 21st Century, however, Gandhi's grandson Arun attributes the saying to the Mahatma, without specifics as to where he heard it said. The Mahatma does seem to have put forward the general idea with "If we could change ourselves, the tendencies in the world would also change. As a man changes his own nature, so does the attitude of the world change towards him."

99 STEP OUTSIDE YOUR COMFORT ZONE

Again, too many possible sources, most of which seem to be motivational speakers.

100 THOSE WHO DO NOT LEARN HISTORY ARE DOOMED TO REPEAT IT

George Santayana most likely coined this adage in his 1905 book *The Life of Reason, Vol. 1* as "Those who cannot remember the past are condemned to repeat it."

101 YOU'LL HAVE TIME

Or so we'd all like to believe.

About the Author

Brad Yung is best known for writing and drawing the alternative comic strip *Stay as you are.*, which appeared in *Geist Magazine*, *Adbusters*, *The WestEnder*, *The Columbia Journal*, *Comic Relief Magazine*, *The Whistler Sea-To-Sky*, *Ricepaper Magazine*, *The Carbondale Times*, and too many underground zines to mention.

He has also been an engineering student, a screenwriter, a toy store clerk, a zinester, a computer programmer, a merchandiser, an actor, a data collection associate, and now an author. He is proud of roughly half of those.

Lessons I'm Going To Teach My Kids Too Late was written over the course of 12 years. It was initially inspired by his time working in a toy store, where one often sees the worst parenting in the world.

He currently resides in Nanaimo, BC, under his new name, 'Harry's dad'.

CPSIA information can be obtained
at www.ICGtesting.com
Printed in the USA
FFHW011841050319
50883075-56286FF